UNDERSTANDING
THE
BIBLE

LAYMAN'S THEOLOGICAL LIBRARY
Robert McAfee Brown, *General Editor*

Modern Rivals to Christian Faith, by Cornelius Loew
The Significance of the Church, by Robert McAfee Brown
Believing in God, by Daniel Jenkins
The Christian Man, by William Hamilton
Prayer and Personal Religion, by John B. Coburn
Life, Death, and Destiny, by Roger L. Shinn
A Faith for the Nations, by Charles W. Forman
Making Ethical Decisions, by Howard Clark Kee
The Meaning of Christ, by Robert Clyde Johnson
Barriers to Belief, by Norman F. Langford
Understanding the Bible, by Fred J. Denbeaux
The Protestant and Politics, by William Lee Miller

*Understanding
the
Bible*

by
Fred J. Denbeaux

LAYMAN'S
THEOLOGICAL
LIBRARY

THE WESTMINSTER PRESS
PHILADELPHIA

Library of Congress Catalog Card No. 58-10218

PRINTED IN THE UNITED STATES OF AMERICA

CONTENTS

Foreword   7

1. A Serious Plea for Lay Scholarship   11
   Casual Acquaintance Versus Serious Study
   Protestantism and the Thrill of Learning
   Learning Involves Listening

2. The Tools of Biblical Study   21
   The Right Kind of " Criticism "
   The First Tool: " Historical Criticism "
   The Second Tool: " Literary Criticism "
   The Church as a Community of Scholars

3. The Church Tries to Understand What God Has Done   31
   The Catholic Churches
   The Protestant Churches
   Sectarian Christianity
   The Bible — and Our Various Traditions

4. The Words of Man and the Word of God (*The Cove-
   nant-Bond*)   42
   The Supreme Importance of Words
   A Word Mutually Pledged
   What Is Required of Man?
   What Is Required of God?
   The Helpless Are Befriended

5. An Ancient Story Which Is Our Story   55
      Being Mature About Maturity
      Not Everyone Felt Comfortable
      Freedom or Slavery: A Hard Choice
      The Unpleasantness of Second Thoughts — and the
        Cost of Freedom
      The Joy and the Risk of Creatureliness
      " Secure " Churches Miss the Point

6. Re-creation and Renewal   70
      The Strangeness of God
      Faith Struggles with Evasions
      The Stumbling Block
      Re-creation and Renewal

   Epilogue: Seeing the World Through the Eyes of the
   Bible   91

FOREWORD

The religious book market is full of books for "the intelligent layman." Some are an insult to his intelligence. Others are covertly written for professional theologians. A few are genuine helps in communicating the faith.

In this spate of books being thrust at the lay reader, what distinctive place can the Layman's Theological Library claim to hold? For one thing, it will try to remind the layman that he *is* a theologian. The close conjunction of the words "layman" and "theological" in the title of the series is not by chance but by design. For theology is not an irrelevant pastime of seminary professors. It is the occupation of every Christian, the moment he begins to think about, or talk about, or communicate, his Christian faith. The injunction to love God *with all his mind,* necessarily involves the layman in theology. He can never avoid theology; if he refuses to think through his faith, he simply settles for an inferior theology.

Furthermore, the Layman's Theological Library will attempt to give a *wholeness* in its presentation of the Christian faith. Its twelve volumes cover the main areas of Christian faith and practice. They are written out of similar convictions which the authors share about the uniqueness of the Christian faith. All the authors are convinced that Christian faith can be made relevant, that it can be made understandable without becoming innocuous, and that (particularly in view of the current "return to religion") it is crucially important for the layman

7

to commit himself to more than "religion in general." The
Layman's Theological Library, then, will attempt a fresh exploration of the Christian faith and what it can mean in the
life of twentieth-century man.

Some small books are written to be skimmed over once and
then put aside. Not so the present volume. For this is a book
that can be read more than once. This is not to say that it cannot be understood after a single reading, but that it is one of
those rare books which will repay repeated reading.

For what the author succeeds in doing is to usher us into
the world of the Bible. This is a world that is a strange world
when compared to our world, and yet it is the only world in
which we can truly find our home. We will be irritated by the
world of the Bible, offended by it, ready more than once, perhaps, to stop trying to understand it. For it is a world that
makes us uneasy. It does not elicit from us the response, "How
nice to discover that the Bible confirms all the things I always
wanted to believe anyhow!" but rather the response: "Oh,
dear, does it *have* to be this way? Why can't I have it on my
own terms?"

Because of the author's unwillingness to give us a Biblical
world transformed into our own world, this is not an ordinary
or conventional book about the Bible. It is more concerned
with our understanding the Bible's central *message* than with
our understanding that there are thirty-nine books in the Old
Testament and twenty-seven in the New. It does not lead us
through book after book. It contains no chronological charts,
no maps, no genealogies, no summaries of battles, no routes of
journeys or migrations. There are other books, good books,
which can furnish these. Instead, this book puts before us the
two main concerns of the Bible — what we will discover to be
called the creation of the covenant-bond between God and his

people, and the later re-creation of that bond. If we have some kind of hold on those things, the chronologies and maps and charts can be seen in their proper perspective.

The author's intent, we shall discover, is to confront us with this main concern of the Bible — how it stands between God and man — and make us see that what happened " back then " is what is happening to us " right now." We are unavoidably obliged to involve ourselves in the Biblical story, to see that " Israel's story " is " our story," and that we cannot deny this fact without denying our own identity.

Another value of this book consists precisely in the fact that it cannot be used as a substitute for reading the Bible itself. This book does not attempt to exhaust, or even summarize, the Bible it is helping the reader to understand. It cannot be read in place of the Bible; it can only force the reader more and more inexorably to that point where he must pick up his Bible and read for himself.

ROBERT McAFEE BROWN

A Serious Plea for Lay Scholarship

The Bible is an exceedingly strange book. It has lent itself for the support of truth and light, and it has also been used to sustain bigotry and darkness. As an ally of culture it has stimulated learning and broadened the horizons of human knowledge. At the same time the defenders of the book have often been so nervous and protective that they have isolated the book from its concern with human affairs, and this is difficult to understand. For what distinguished the faith of the Bible from other ancient faiths was the conviction that God and justice were inseparable, and that God was being worshiped only in so far as the needs of individuals and society were being met. Thus the magnificent statement, which is the ground of all personal freedom: " You shall have one law for the sojourner and for the native; for I am the Lord your God." (Lev. 24:22.)

In spite of the " involvement " of God in our common life, untold numbers of readers have presumed that the Bible is largely a collection of doctrines about religion. Indeed not! In the Bible, God is concerned with every dimension of human existence. So Calvin attacked, in his day, those " expressly denying the existence of God; not that they deprive God of his being, but because they rob him of his justice and providence, shutting him up as an idler in heaven " (*Institutes* I. iv.2).

While these people have been making God an "idler in heaven," other "students" of the Bible have used the Bible to justify oppression and injustice. Thus, in our day the Bible is still being used to "justify" white supremacy. The Bible, unless it is understood carefully, can become a cruelly dangerous book. It is both the father of knowledge and the mother of superstition.

The Bible is an enigmatic book. It is the central support of a great religious tradition. The members of that tradition, however, have always found the book confusing. The Christian church believes that the Bible reflects a unique revelation from God. The individual within that church may respect, fear, venerate, and even worship the Bible. Understand it, however, he does not. This is not because he is incapable of understanding. But the Bible is a book so difficult that from the outset it should be said that it is unreadable. Any reader who sits down in simplicity of heart and integrity of purpose soon finds that his reading is interrupted. He cannot understand the strange customs, digressions, and burdensome details which obscure the theme as well as fog the interest. What sensible reason can there be for the statement that the Lord tried to kill Moses and that he was put off by an act of circumcision? (Ex. 4:24-26.) Why on earth does Elisha need a minstrel before he can prophesy? (II Kings 3:15.)

Of course, it can be argued, there are still people who *do* read the Bible. Perhaps they do, but many of them refuse to allow their minds to become involved. They ask no questions of the material. They remember everything and understand nothing. They occasionally become participants on quiz shows and win fortunes because they know "facts" about the Bible. But they still have not really read, because they have not grappled with the underlying questions that the Bible puts to the reader. Nor have they, apart from amassing information, un-

derstood what the text is trying to say in relation to the background of the writer. They have understood little and what
they have learned has little depth.

Casual Acquaintance Versus Serious Study

Genuine reading, however, does involve comprehension. We
will come closer to the message of the Bible if we recognize
that what is needed is less casual reading and more serious
study.

In all the great and complex areas of human culture, understanding requires discipline. In music and painting, for example, truth is not easily come by. What is the difference between
a Li'l Abner cartoon and a Picasso painting? What is the difference between "popular" music and Mozart's *Jupiter* symphony? Neither the cartoon nor the popular music requires
much from the observer or the listener. The humor of a cartoon and the rhythm of a show song are obvious. They require
no study: their meaning is self-evident. Picasso and Mozart,
on the other hand, require that the viewer and the listener
engage seriously in their observation. We don't "understand"
Picasso's *Guernica* by seeing it once. Similarly, the more we
study — really study — the *Jupiter* symphony, the more meaning it has. That the fourth movement is an involved fugue
may be irrelevant to the dilettante, but to the person who
wants to "understand" the music, it is immensely important.
In short, the difference here is between "easy reading" and
study. In the same sense, the Bible is a book so complex, so
infinitely rich, that it cannot be read: it must be studied.

The Bible is not a simple book. It is an anthology or collection of writings which were created over a twelve-hundred-
year period. It is a book that reflects many different kinds of
history, and if the reader is impatient with history, he will

have great difficulty understanding the Bible. The Bible, furthermore, contains many different types of *literature*. If a
person is unwilling to make literary distinctions, to differenti-
ate between prose and poetry, historical narrative and myth,
he will not really comprehend the rich world of the Bible.

It is unfortunate that so many Americans have assumed an
anti-intellectual pose. Among such people there is a feeling
that history and literature are insignificant. With Henry Ford,
many will believe that "history is bunk." For these people, it
would have been better if God had chosen to reveal himself
in some reality other than a book about history. Unfortunately
for those who are impatient with disciplines of the mind, God
did choose to communicate himself through a book, and a very
complex book at that. The person who is unwilling to study,
unwilling to understand both history and literature, cannot
understand the Bible. It would be helpful if such a person
could turn on an electronic machine that would go through
the labor that understanding requires, and perhaps give it to
him subliminally. He could, in the meantime, enjoy himself.
Unfortunately for such a person, the only instrument that can
understand the stuff of history and literature is the human
mind. . . .

Protestantism and the Thrill of Learning

The Bible is both a dangerous and a difficult book. However,
there are safeguards to protect us against the dangers, and
methods to enable us to overcome the difficulties. The Protestant tradition from the very beginning has been aware of the
problems that beset interpretation. The Protestant doctrine of
"the priesthood of all believers" commits the tradition to a
nonauthoritarian form of knowing. The priesthood of all believers, a classical Reformation doctrine, means among other

things that each believer is himself responsible for his relationship to God. No priest, no clergyman, no ecclesiastical system can be a substitute for full personal knowledge and involvement. This means that, for the Protestant, the understanding of the Bible cannot be delegated to priests, evangelists, or specialists. The vision underlying the Protestant faith is not fulfilled until the tools of learning are made available to the average man. It is for this reason that the Protestant faith has always been a vigorous ally of public education. A mind intellectually depressed cannot be spiritually uplifted.

There is a relationship between Protestantism, high standards of education, and the fact that God communicated himself through a *book*. The Roman Catholic tradition speaks differently. There, the center is not in the book but in the sacramental Mass, a profound liturgical drama in which the priest is central. Just as the mark of the Protestant culture is a high standard of education, so the mark of a Roman Catholic culture is liturgical and ecumenical richness. Much of the liturgical poverty of Protestantism is due, not to a nonaesthetic temperament, but to the fact that our energies have gone into the creation of schools instead of cathedrals. In the hope that the mind of the average man would cease to be average, we Protestants have chosen to become liturgical mendicants.

As Protestants we must therefore fulfill the mission entrusted to us. We must be serious about the life and nurture of the mind. We must not retreat from our peculiar vision. If a carpenter can put on a roof that will not leak, he can understand the structure that goes into a book. If a businessman can run his business so that he does justice to his employees, taxes, and his own interests, he can understand the complex nature of the Bible. A boy whose mind is good enough to build an airplane model and make it fly has a mind capable of understanding the problems of scholarship. Scholarship is not something apart, a strange and fearful discipline. Scholarship is simply a way of being careful with the material. Just as one tries to use saw and hammer correctly so that the wood will do what is wanted, so too does the scholar use the tools of his mind to make the book yield its meaning. In both cases carefulness is required. A good carpenter knows the nature of wood. Anyone can splinter wood, but it takes a craftsman to work according to the law of the wood. In the same fashion anyone can manipulate a book, but it takes a craftsman to understand the book in order to force it to surrender its meaning. And Protestantism makes the gamble that in this sense we can all be craftsmen.

Everything has its structure, and we can work with that structure only if we are willing to submit ourselves to a discipline. If the Protestant tradition takes itself seriously, it will encourage us to appropriate the disciplines that will produce knowledge. The church has quite wrongly permitted the Bible to become the property of specialists and clergymen. We educate a few people to be " Biblical scholars " on the assumption that they will tell the rest of us what the Bible is about. Religion will always seem a little vague and unreal until the " average " man has sought and found *for himself* answers that must come from his own intellectual development. It is not the function of the church to " pass on information." It is very much the responsibility of the church to make learning so attractive that no one will want to remain ignorant.

But Protestantism today has become the haven of easy religion. The figure who most symbolizes Protestantism today is the evangelist. We have seen not only the illiterate but the leaders of churches flock to the support of " old-time religion." The evangelist appears in a filled arena, the crowd is excited as the leader speaks, cries, prays, thumps, jumps, turns, stares, points, shouts, and whispers. The crowd is hypnotized because it knows that the answer will be given. But it is an answer that involves no search, no struggle, no enlightenment on the part of the audience. It is to our shame that when people are crying for knowledge we give them the cheap excitement of an authoritarian answer instead.

From this kind of obscurantism we need to be delivered. We cannot carry water on both shoulders. We cannot educate men and at the same time make them dependent upon high-pressure personalities. Just as Protestantism cannot communicate its view of the Bible by imitating the Roman Catholic Church, so also it cannot surrender to those who substitute emotional excitement for the discipline of study. Protestantism holds that God's truth cannot come to any individual unless he is himself willing to make the sacrifice that truth demands. Each man must grapple for himself with all the problems that give meaning to learning.

This, of course, is asking a great deal. It is asking not only for time but also for discipline in a period when our intellectual muscles have deteriorated. Yet as Protestants we must hold to this more rigorous course because we are convinced that the man who refuses the quick and easy answers will, in the process of learning, gain a dignity that he would not otherwise possess.

But this concern must not degenerate into cheap individualism, each person merely claiming " the truth as he sees it." We need to remember that the Protestant tradition is not without form. We are not free to do as we please. We believe that God has communicated himself through a book to a church that is equipped to understand his speech. God is neither unknown nor silent. God speaks to men and women whose intelligence and perceptivity are strengthened by the fact that God spoke. God's communication is through speech — through words and not through meaningless sounds. The sounds that we hear from eternity are the words of our Creator and not the aimless gibberish of a cosmic idiot. It is necessary, therefore, that we begin to think again of human beings as *those whom God has addressed*. It will be the task of the church to see to it that men and women dare to believe in themselves. Vested with confidence, they will employ tools and disciplines that they thought were beyond themselves. They will encounter what every man must know if he is truly human — the thrill of learning.

Learning Involves Listening

The iron logic of Protestantism demands that men shall be transformed from casual readers into serious students of the Bible. The Bible is a book that demands our complete attention. It cannot be classified as " vacation reading." It is a book for mature minds.

There is, of course, a place for easy reading. There are all kinds of light books that can be read without the mind's alert activity. Similarly, there are all kinds of records that can be described as background music. One listens to such music effortlessly. If one of Bach's Brandenberg concertos were to be slipped onto a pile of " easy listening " music, the listener would receive a mental shock. The concerto would make demands upon the understanding that the lazy mind could not answer. The Bible is a book analogous to " demanding " music. We can listen to it only with full attention.

How is God understood? The word of God is not a background noise. God's speech is not for easy listening. When God speaks, he speaks to the total personality. Our hearts, our wills, and our minds are involved. We depreciate the dignity and the complexity of human existence if we neglect our intelligence. Although each one of us has intellectual limits, it is also true that most of us have failed to push ourselves to that limit.

So Protestantism is a "hard" and not a "soft" faith. It is built upon rigorous thinking and careful study. As Protestants, we are crucially concerned with the life of the mind. Unlike animals, we live in a world vibrantly alive wtih communication. Through symbols, words, music, and colors we learn something of how other people live on the inside of their lives. Thus a book, a painting, or a piece of music is a refreshing experience because it enables us to leave the prison of our own solitude and enter into the deep experience of others.

There is, therefore, a clear connection between God's providence and the development of an individual or people. As the child and the people develop, they leave the primitive world of taste and smell and enter into the nuances of thought and profound communication. As words are learned, humanity increases. We know how much we are restricted in our humanity if we cannot communicate ourselves. We also know how much we are enriched if we can understand what others are telling us. Each of us can remember the embarrassment of having tried and having failed to say what we really meant. We also, one hopes, can remember the thrill we felt when we found just the right words to communicate our meaning. A child, through words and other symbols, becomes human. A people, through music and painting and thought, become cultured. Only as a child becomes mature and only as a people submit to understanding can either understand a God who has chosen ⸀o communicate through words.

This same movement from immaturity to maturity is experienced by the people of the Bible, the Israelites. As every Sunday school child knows, the story tells us that God first *spoke words* to the Bible people when they were nomads. Still on the edge of primitivism, they did not always have enough command of language to do justice to their encounter with God. Yet God chose these slaves at the precise moment when

Israel was moving out of primitivism into maturity. Israel on the verge of political and literary life, Israel moving out of narrow tribalism into the community of nations, became the recipient of God's special communication. Had he chosen to speak to the blood ancestors of some of these people five thousand years earlier, he would have spoken to brutes who could neither have understood nor have had the skills to retain and record the message.

As individuals we find ourselves in exactly the same situation. We must determine whether we are to behave as brutes in the presence of God or whether, moving out of our own twilight zones, we are prepared to do God the courtesy of listening to him, not only with full attention, but with the most fully developed minds that we can cultivate. If the latter, we shall not be afraid to learn, we shall not be afraid to discipline our minds.

Only in such a manner can we know Him and understand ourselves.

2

THE TOOLS OF BIBLICAL STUDY

If we decide to take seriously the opportunity — and the risk — of using our minds, more is needed than simply the bare decision to do so. Certain skills must be developed if we are to be responsible " lay scholars."

This need not be as intimidating as it sounds. Obviously a layman gives the major portion of his time to carpentry, law, advertising, personnel, schoolteaching, or whatever may be the area in which he earns his living. He cannot devote full time to Biblical study, nor does he need to, for he does not have to begin from scratch. He has available, in translation, the text of the Bible, and with this in hand there are some problems he *can* leave to the " experts." He need not be overly concerned with the original languages or, for example, with the problems of the *canon* (the debate over which writings were to be considered " sacred "), or with problems of *textual criticism* (concerning the agreements and disagreements in the ancient handwritten copies of the books of the Bible). *Archaeology* he can read or not as he pleases, since the conclusions of this branch of knowledge affecting faith have necessarily been subjective. (Witness the continuing furor over what the Dead Sea scrolls mean.)

The Right Kind of " Criticism "

There are really only two areas of study that need to concern the lay Biblical scholar. These are the disciplines of
(1) historical criticism and (2) literary criticism. Before looking at the adjectives, let us examine the noun.

What is " criticism "? Criticism involves a rational and a
questioning approach to the material being studied. Note especially that it is not directly related to the question of belief or
unbelief, and that rather than represent an attempt to be destructive, it represents a constructive approach to the material.
One must question, one must be " critical," whether one believes or not. The difference between a critical and a noncriti-
cal approach is an extremely important difference. It is the
difference between actively understanding what one believes
and passively accepting it.

Picture a young worker being instructed for the first time
in the operation of a lathe. The foreman, a teacher, explains as
the young man listens, absorbing information. After the foreman has finished his demonstration the young worker is given
time to ask questions. It is at this point that he becomes a
" critic." By asking questions, he shows the alertness of his
mind and his willingness to learn. It is only after his own
mind has become active in this way that he is prepared to use
the machine intelligently.

A student stands in exactly the same relation to the world
of books. The books also must be understood with an alert
mind. It is only after the student begins to ask hard and
" critical " questions that his own understanding begins to
function. Without criticism and questions, the mind does not
come alive. Unless the mind is alive it is not a true instrument
of understanding.

Criticism must be honest. It reveals that the scholar is a seeker instead of a knower. Criticism is a method by which the student admits his initial ignorance. Those who are clever about hiding their ignorance are unable to learn. A penalty must be paid for such pretension. If the young factory worker pretends rather than learns, it will not be long before he will be turning out defective pieces with the lathe.

A student finds himself in a similar relation to a book. He must ask the questions which the understanding requires, questions like: "What were the conditions under which this curious story was written?" or "What did the author have in mind when he wrote this?" If the student does not ask honest questions soon, he will be extracting defective answers from the book. For instance, if a reader never asks the question, "Why are there two stories of the creation in Genesis?" he will be missing the drama of a developing faith and limiting himself to a merely surface reading.

It takes courage for a man to be critical, for in doing so the man reveals his own ignorance. But this is the *only* way a man can learn. He does not pretend that he already knows what the book says. Nor does he force the book to say what will make him comfortable. Rather, *he yields to the book,* whether it makes him comfortable or not. The process of learning always involves pain since it reminds the learner of his own incompleteness. Minds that are willing to grow will, however, trust the critical process, for they know that it is the road to truth. The lay scholar, then, must not be afraid to be a "critic," for he must realize that far from being destructive, such an approach is the only honestly constructive approach there is.

The First Tool: "Historical Criticism"

Let us now go on to distinguish the two kinds of criticism
the lay scholar must have at his disposal. The first of these is
historical criticism.

To begin with, if we are really to understand the history
and literature of the Bible, we must have the courage to read
the Bible directly. It would be easier, but quite misleading, if
we were to read someone else's interpretation of it, and the
present book is expressly designed to prevent the Bible's being
used this way. Just as it is impossible to develop one's shoulder
muscles by hiring another person to do push-ups, so too is it
impossible to develop one's intellectual muscles by hiring a
scholar to " explain " the Bible to us.

Where, then, do we begin? The answer is not so difficult.
We must begin with the people who created the literature.
This point may seem so obvious as to sound stupid. But the
point must be made. Until a literature has been created we can
only see a silent people. To a large extent this is true of the
Stone Age man, for example. Men of the Stone Age may have
felt and hoped, but what they felt and hoped we shall never
know, for they left us no words, no literature.

The people who produced the Bible were not, however, a
silent people. They had passed out of the Stone Age and entered into the Bronze and perhaps the Iron Age. The Hebrews
who produced the book we know as the Bible were, most critical thinkers are convinced, also in an agricultural rather than in
a sheepherding economy. This means that the writers of early
Hebrew literature had ceased to be nomads.

From this it follows that Abraham, Isaac, and Jacob (and
for that matter, Moses) could not have been the creators of
our Bible. These early shepherds may have told stories around
the campfire but they did not create literature. It is for this

reason, perhaps, that Abraham and Moses seem to be a little
" vague " to most readers. We know very little of their " inner "
lives.

It is not until we meet the Hebrews in Palestine and see
them borrowing " civilized " tools from their neighbors that
we really meet " flesh and blood " people. It is no accident that
among all the " early " heroes David is the most real to us. As
we read his story, a story that shows inner feelings as well as
outward acts, we cannot help feeling that the writers knew
and loved him. David's kingdom is, for the first time, a " set-
tled " kingdom. No longer shepherds, no longer on the move,
David and his people are able to learn the arts and crafts that
make it possible, for the first time, to put into written form
some of the ancient tales.

Borrowing from older and more literary peoples (the Phoeni-
cians and the Philistines), the Hebrews learned how to write,
how to use words, how to spin out their dreams, how to say
what they meant. Out of this new discovery, empowered by
language, they spoke of their origins — whence they had come
and why.

What we learn about Abraham and Moses, for instance, we
must learn not through their own eyes but through the eyes
of those who lived hundreds of years later, the men who, in
the times of David and Solomon, began to put into written
form some of the ancient campfire tales. It is in the time of
David and Solomon that the Hebrew begins to put things together, begins to reflect on meanings, begins to express some
concern about the significance of national life. It is in this
period, around 1000–900 B.C., that portions of our Bible came
into being as written documents. In the beginning much of
the material was fragmentary: not for another hundred or
more years did it seem necessary for anyone to weave the
pieces together.

A modern reader, trying to understand the history that

helped produce the Bible, would do well to read some of this early literature, the stories of the origin of the monarchy in I and II Samuel and, in Gen. 2:4 to 4:25, the story of the Creation as it was told by a writer shortly after the time of David. Once this world of David and Solomon is understood, the modern reader will have gone far toward applying *historical analysis* to the " stories " of Abraham, Isaac, and Jacob, and the faith that understood life in terms of the Creation and the exodus.

The Second Tool: " Literary Criticism "

The second tool for Bible study, *literary criticism,* is concerned with the actual records left by a civilization. What kind of records did the Hebrews leave? Fortunately for us, they left the most exciting of all messages, literature. They left us their journals, their poetry, their epics, the records of their kings — all interwoven in the book that we know as the Bible.

The messages left for posterity are of the most intimate kind. The literature was not written to be " shown," as a schoolboy might write an essay to impress his teachers. Little effort is made to censor the literature. Kings are, on the whole, described for what they were — some good, some bad, most both. The literature is not the kind of " improving " literature usually written for Sunday schools. Rather, it is compounded out of the raw material of life. It is a story of good kings who do bad things (David and Solomon). It is a story of ordinary men compelled against their will to proclaim the unpopular message of God (Moses and Amos). It is a story of men who can both bless the Lord and curse the day of their birth (Jeremiah and Job).

What, we may ask, goes on in literary criticism? This kind

of criticism is concerned with finding out what a person means by the way in which he says it. We all know that in ordinary conversation it is important to determine not only *what* is said but also *how* it is said. Thus, in many Southern states, it is the custom to say to a friend or acquaintance, " Come and see us." This " word " is simply an expression of Southern politeness and cannot be taken literally: it is a gracious way of saying good-by.

Literary criticism is simply the application of common sense to literature, as must be done every day in conversation. Literary criticism thus concerns itself with the way in which words are used. An ancient writer uses words in different ways to convey different meanings. We must try to know, for instance, whether the writer is telling us of an event that he has witnessed, or whether he is trying to get at the meaning *behind* some event. Thus not all events really happen: sometimes an " event " is an illustration of some truth that is intended to give purpose and direction to a story.

For example, in the story of Jacob and Bethel (Gen. 28:10-22), we are told that the Lord appears to Jacob in a dream and so impressed was Jacob that, upon awaking, he named the place Bethel, which means " house of God." The writer of this story did not take the story literally. It was, rather, a " word " by which he reinterpreted the significance of a shrine at the town of Bethel. Around 900 B.C., this " shrine " was a place where foreign gods (or Baals) were being worshiped. What the writer is doing is telling his own generation (900 B.C.) that the God who is being worshiped there is not really a Baal, but actually is the ancient tribal God of Jacob and Abraham. By this story the author woos his readers away from the Canaanite Baals (who had been worshiped at Bethel) and " claims " the shrine for the living Lord of the Hebrews. This tells us that one of the ancient methods by which a writer suggested a "meaning" was to describe the happening in terms of a dream.

The lay scholar who asks persistent questions of the material will soon find that there are other literary forms to be distinguished. Soon he will learn to distinguish between court records (II Sam. 8:15-18) and epic prose (Gen., chs. 12 and 13).

On another level he will sense that words are not used the same in narrative prose as they are in poetry. What do we expect from the words of narrative prose? We expect a story that will tell us the sequence of events as they happened. So in II Sam. 15:1 to 19:8 we read a dramatic and moving account of Absalom's unsuccessful rebellion against his father, King David. We have only to read the story to "feel" that we are being confronted with the account of an actual revolution.

If we turn from the creative journalism of narrative prose to *poetry,* we discover that poetry gives quite a different meaning to words. We are not really asked to believe that "the morning stars sang together" (Job 38:7) or that "the sun stood still, and the moon stayed" (Josh. 10:13), but that in both cases the writers are using poetic license to declare, in cosmic terms, the identity of the ruler of the universe.

Careful reading soon shows the reader that writers frequently use poetry, legends, and myths to get at dimensions of truth deeper than can be gotten at through matter-of-fact prose. The reader will need to develop his own way of expressing the differences in the literary forms. If we look, for instance, at the first chapter of Genesis, we must ask ourselves: "What kind of literature is this? Is it close to journalism? Is it supposed to be an eyewitness account of something that can be discussed as a historical event? Is it closer to poetry? Is the writer doing more than telling about something that happened? Is he 'getting at' a truth regarding the ultimate meaning of life?" Only as we learn to make such distinctions can we be fair to the intention of the original writers. Being fair is the goal of *literary criticism.*

This may sound difficult. It is. Every shift from intellectual laziness to alertness is painful. Fortunately it is possible to change one's habits. It is possible even for those in their middle years to learn to appreciate music. It is also possible to learn to read critically, to join the company of those who are trying to understand the Bible, not in a primitive or childish fashion, but with maturity of mind.

The Church as a Community of Scholars

In order for us to begin a serious study of what the Bible is about we must examine, not only the Bible, but also a number of related problems. We shall want to examine some of the most important Biblical themes. We shall want to know about God's covenant with man (Chapters 4 and 5), man's dependency upon grace and how both covenant and grace help us to live as creatures (Chapter 6). Also we must at least raise the questions: What is the relation of the Bible to other books? What is the relation of the Bible to culture in general (Epilogue)?

But before doing these things there is one other task we must face. We must pay some attention, not only to the Bible, but also to our own minds, and to our own heritage. How do we begin "understanding the Bible"? Do we begin from scratch? Do we begin as Protestants? as Catholics? as neither? How can we get rid of the obstructions in our vision?

Since we are a part of a community — the church — we must look at ways in which that community has sought to interpret the Bible. The presence of this community can be a help as well as a hindrance. One of the joys of scholarship is that it involves community effort. The layman will find, in addition to the help he may get from libraries, that his minister will be glad to share some of his own training. The clergyman hungers for a community of minds. He needs the stimulation that he cannot get from the somewhat frenzied organizational life of the church. He, too, struggles to keep his mind alive and he will welcome concern in this area from the members of his congregation. He knows that the church is only really the church when there is a rich intellectual and spiritual interchange between the pulpit and the pew. Without lay scholarship the pews might as well be empty. With it, a true community can emerge.

But there are problems here as well, problems significant enough to have a chapter to themselves.

lown to them or serve them; for I the Lord your God am
ious God." (Ex. 20:4-5.)

critical and creaturely participants in the church, we must
ys resist rigidity, because such inflexibility always repre-
the creation of a " graven image," which is precisely the
station against which the First Commandment warns.

ith regard to the use of the Bible in the " Catholic tradi-
," the danger always is that instead of judging the tradi-
, the Bible will be " used " by the tradition to justify its
position. That judgment begins " with the household of
d " is a part of the Biblical message that can rather easily
overlooked. It is the unique task of the Protestant tradition
remind each communion within Christendom that God's
ord is a judgment on all our pretensions.

The Protestant Churches

If Protestants have failed to do justice to Catholic tradition
nd God's continuous involvement with post-Biblical affairs,
must also be said that Catholicism has failed to do justice
the significance of the original revelation, and the written
ecord in Scripture by which that revelation had been com-
nunicated to succeeding generations. If the Catholic church
has been the custodian of tradition, Protestantism has been
he champion of a faith centered in the Bible.

By calling attention again and again to the Bible, Protestantism reminds Christendom that there was a *word* uttered which
is quite different from our varying theologies and our separate
ecclesiastical traditions. Thus there is provided an assurance
that Methodists and Presbyterians and Roman Catholics and
Greek Orthodox can find a point at which to meet. It cannot
be expected that a Roman Catholic would ever be comfortable

CHAPTER

3

THE CHURCH TRIES TO UNDERSTAND WHAT GOD HAS DONE

We have, then, the Bible, but we do not have the Bible
all by itself. We have the Bible and the church, or more precisely, we have the Bible and *various* churches, all of which
do various things with the Bible.

We cannot escape the problem this raises. Rather, we must
seek to understand it. The purpose of the present chapter is
to seek such understanding, and to provide us with some
further perspective as we seek, for ourselves, to understand
the Bible.

The church communicates a faith that it frequently corrupts
and that it usually misunderstands. The church is not the
light; it is rather an instrument through which that light is
communicated to the world. The church must remember that
" whoever would save his life will lose it; and whoever loses
his life for my sake and the gospel's will save it " (Mark 8:35).

All churches face the same problem: How can one be a
messenger of the Most High and still maintain humility?
How can one, as it were, "represent" God and still have a
sense of one's own limitations? The church finds itself em-

barrassed by this high task. To cover its embarrassment it dons an uncreaturely mask. The church soon adjusts itself to the role of a proud warrior. It forgets that it was meant to be a humble creature. Thus it is that when any church faces any other church it seeks to escape its own limits by assuming a superiority of antiquity or revelation, a superiority that could never be justified by the good news of a crucified Messiah.

The churches, which, in their own special ways, alternate between trembling creatureliness and pretentious conviction, can be roughly divided into three families: (1) The Roman and the Anglican churches find their authority primarily in tradition, liturgy, and the sacraments. (2) The Protestant and Reformed churches are supported largely by a Biblical and Confessional faith. (3) Sectarian Christians are those who place most emphasis on the fulfillment of the Christian life that comes through the Holy Spirit.

We must look at them in turn and see how they relate themselves to the Bible we are here seeking to understand.

The Catholic Churches

The Catholic churches, whether Roman or Anglican, are basically concerned with tradition, with the community's liturgical participation in the drama of that tradition, and with the sacramental power by which God's redemptive force is communicated. Catholicism stresses the fact that the community which God founded in Abraham, the community which has been extended into the Gentile world (the church), is still a separate and peculiar community. It is a community which has its own marks, which has a destiny quite different from the destinies of other communities. It is a community which, as Augustine suggested, will outlive every empire, for

it is a community bonded to eternity.

Protestantism has much to learn from
ants are frequently insensitive to the fac
working through both Israel and Christen
turies. As a result Protestants are often
neutral toward, that history in which G
significant Protestant theologian of the 1
Kierkegaard, inadvertently stated the weak
ant position when he said that a Christian is
two moments, the moment of the incarnatio
lar moment in which the Christian happens
somewhat barren view does not do justice
with human history since the time of Abraha
that God has been directing history since the
the Bible was written. Catholicism more tr
God's continuing and intimate concern for h
the beginning, through each stage, and until th
We Protestants therefore need to criticize our
terest in tradition and history, for we have
from the Catholic appreciation of history under

At the same time, the Protestant must be a
and uneasy about the uncreaturely pride that i
particular views of tradition by the Catholic ch
claim for a fixed and final authority for an Epi
tion, or for the supremacy of the Roman bishop,
seen as departures from finitude and creaturelines
dom, on the whole, has resisted every attempt to
any single form of government because of the imp
the First Commandment.

"You shall not make yourself a graven image, or
ness of anything that is in heaven above, or that is in
beneath, or that is in the water under the earth; you

with the content of a Lutheran culture. Nor will many Methodists, nurtured on a religion of the heart, find much help in so abstract a thinker as Thomas Aquinas. As a result, there must be some "home ground" on which all our traditions can meet. This will surely be in that world to which *all* our traditions are responses, the world of the Bible, God's speech and the human record thereof.

The Bible is the assurance that we shall have some common standards by which to judge our own theologies and confessions. The fact that there is a Bible that in some sense transcends all the ecclesiastical traditions is a reminder that we must distinguish between God's word and human interpretations. Lutherans, Presbyterians, Catholics, and Baptists must remember that *our* thought is partially a distortion of *Another's* speech. Our hope is not in ourselves but in that word from beyond which binds us together. The Bible is the assurance that that word has been spoken as a check upon our own inventiveness.

Just as Catholicism represents Christendom's concern with the continuity of tradition, so Protestantism represents a concern with the *beginning* of that tradition. Our history began and it will end: we are not on a treadmill. Because God entered time, because his word lodged among us, all the succeeding generations have lived differently. That God chose to "begin" us cannot be forgotten, and as Protestants we are aware of the mystery of our beginning. We know that there was a time when we were not, when the Voice had not yet been heard, a time when all humanity might have said with T. E. Lawrence, "There is an ideal standard somewhere and only that matters, and I cannot find it." But history now has purpose in that the standard has become a Voice. We no longer perch wearily upon a merry-go-round since God spoke to Abraham. Our appreciation for the Bible helps us to get at the mystery of our origin, reminds us that something *really* happened, that God started something and that we are a part of the process which he began. The Bible is the assurance that our times and our children's times are significant, because God broke into time and placed it under his jurisdiction.

As Protestants, we are also aware of the fact that the Bible contains a specific moral content. This is to say that in the prophets and in Jesus we read of life that is immeasurably truer than the lives that we actually do lead. Traditions tend to be bent according to the way people want to live. For example, the tradition that, in popular language, we call " the American way of life," represents the way in which Americans have bent their view of morality to fit their own desires. But the Bible is not so easily bent. Although its content is not always transparent, still there is a sense in which, whether as Catholics or Protestants or Americans, we are brought to a sharp halt when we are reminded that God is not a God of human convenience but a God of judgment as well as of love. The Catholic church, Protestant theologians, and secular patriots may attempt to convince us that killing is justified under some circumstances; but meanwhile it is helpful to remember that Jesus said: " You have heard that it was said, ' You shall love your neighbor and hate your enemy.' But I say to you, Love your enemies and pray for those who persecute you." By such a word as this we are reminded of a moral demand that cannot be erased for our convenience. The Bible thus is an assurance that we will not get lost in our own words and rationalizations.

Sectarian Christianity

Like the Protestants and the Catholics, the Sectarians also are concerned with the Bible. If the Catholics tend to bend the Bible to meet the demands of tradition, the Sectarians tend to bend the Bible to fit their principles of selectivity. This means that the Sectarian does not struggle with the whole Bible, but rather extracts those passages which tend to support his own " gospel."

What is the Sectarian gospel? It is a gospel not grounded in liturgy, sacraments, or even Biblical preaching, but concerned primarily with Christian living. It places an almost total emphasis upon conscience and man's moral obligation to his neighbor. What distinguishes the Sectarian gospel from both the Catholic and Protestant gospel is the overriding conviction that the Christian life can be lived *now,* that there is no need to postpone complete obedience to God.

The Catholic is related to God most magnificently in the sacramental act. Before the body and blood of Jesus Christ he finds himself truly in the presence of God. The Protestant finds himself in the presence of God most significantly when the Biblical word of judgment and mercy in the sermon lifts him out of the world of his " convenience " and confronts him with the explosive crisis of God. The Sectarian, by contrast, finds his most significant moment in neither sacrament nor sermon (these may even be omitted) but in an act of complete obedience.

The emphasis upon obedience, the *now* of faith, indicates a victory over sin that implies special divine help. Thus the Sectarian, facing the problem of conscience, believes that the essence of the Christian tradition is expressed in the coming of the Holy Spirit, a Spirit who comes with *power* and thereby enables man to fulfill the divine will.

We can best understand the spirit of the Sectarian mind by looking at an example. Francis of Assisi, a thirteenth-century Christian, became dramatically and personally involved with the demand of faith upon reading Matt. 10:7-10: " And preach as you go, saying, ' The kingdom of heaven is at hand.' Heal the sick, raise the dead, cleanse lepers, cast out demons. You received without pay, give without pay. Take no gold, nor silver, nor copper in your belts, no bag for your journey, nor two tunics, nor sandals, nor a staff. . . ." And so the gospel of Francis became a gospel of joyful poverty. His Christ was the naked and poor Messiah. In casting the gospel in terms of poverty he appealed to the conscience of an age that had grown weary of the wealth and magnificence of the churches.

Like Francis, the Sectarians are primarily concerned with a victory over the evils that bind men to hunger and bloodshed. Generally opposed to either war or economic and social inequality, and sometimes both, they believe that the Lord Christ sent the Spirit in order that — literally — swords would be beaten into plowshares and spears into pruning hooks. They are also convinced that no man has a right to luxury or security as long as a brother has need. Refusing to slay any brother, they are generally pacifists; refusing to hold private property, they are sometimes socialists. These people, so much as the world allows them, live according to the gospel of pure love.

Both Protestants and Catholics have something to learn from the Sectarian conscience. When we measure ourselves by the Sectarian conscience, we discover that we have all compromised too much. The Sectarian conscience makes it necessary for us to be uneasy as we practice *our* politics and *our* economics; and through the purity of their vision we know how far we are from the Kingdom of God. Of what point is the Catholic sacrament if it does not alert men to the disharmony of their lives with God's will? Of what purpose is vigorous Protestant preaching if its judgments do not help to create new solutions to the ethical and moral dilemmas of our day? The Sectarian reminds us that we must not retreat into either the sermon or the sacrament, but that we must move out from both sermon and sacrament into newness of life.

At the same time, the Sectarian must be reminded that he has been unduly selective and that he has thereby oversimplified the Bible. It is true that the Bible emphasizes the gift of the Spirit, and from this we may conclude that we could do infinitely more works of conscience than we actually do. At the same time the Bible also points to the fact that the Christian must live dependently and hopefully, knowing that his life will not be fulfilled until the return of the Messiah. There is a sense in which the Sectarian conscience is moralistic and separatistic. The Sectarian can become so concerned with the purity of *his* life that he all but secedes from the human race. He sets up a community outside of normal historical communities, and is sometimes a little harsh on the Catholics and the Protestants who have, for the sake of the relevancy of Christ's love, chosen to remain within the " corruptions " of nations and empires.

The Bible — and Our Various Traditions

Here, then, are three great streams in Christian history. A few readers of this book may belong to the first, and a few more will belong to the third. Most will be part of the second. Is the answer, as we struggle with " understanding the Bible," simply to adopt the second or Protestant position? No, it is not. The answer is a little more complex, and we must now look at it for a few moments.

How *are* we to understand the Bible? We will not understand the Bible by bending it to fit our traditions — as Catholicism tends to do. Nor will we understand the Bible by separating it from its continuity in historical traditions — as Protestantism tends to do. Nor can we understand the Bible if we ignore its radical challenge to conscience — as the Sectarian

protest reminds us that we all do. The answer to our question
is quite plain.

We can get to the Bible only through Catholic *and* Protestant
and Sectarian insights. If we choose one and not the others,
we will find ourselves slightly " inventive " (Catholic), nar-
rowly literalistic (Protestant), or mildly fanatic (Sectarian).
None of these is a happy choice. But there is a choice superior
to any single one of these. It is the choice of " understanding
the Bible " through the three traditions together. The Protestant
emphasis upon the ancient record of revelation must be related
to the Catholic view of the richness of Christian history. The
record must be understood in the light of tradition (Catholicism's concern) while every effort is made to see that tradition
does not corrupt the ancient record (Protestantism's concern).
At the same time the Bible is not a morally neutral book, and
we can be reminded by Quakers, Anabaptists, and other sectarian groups of the relevance of the gospel for our social and
personal lives. If God's revelation to humanity in the Bible is
to be understood aright, we must take seriously the witness of
Protestantism, Catholicism, and Sectarianism. We must be
something of each in order that we can understand the Bible
in terms of, respectively, its original *record,* its post-Biblical
tradition, and the dynamic of its *conscience.* We must take
seriously, as Protestantism does, the especial power and validity
of the Biblical record in which God's voice and his dialogue
with man was " recorded." But we must also simultaneously
give heed to the way in which our fathers before us have tried
to interpret that record, and we must finally recognize that the
Holy Spirit is still alive, encouraging us to find new ways of
making the gospel of Jesus Christ concrete.

We would all find it easier to live with a single comfortable
idea, whether *just* the ancient record, *just* the traditions of the
church, or *just* the Holy Spirit. Sin is always easy, and faith

means daring to be uncomfortable in the hope that God can teach us. So, He who makes us human first makes us uncomfortable.

These are the terms on which we can attempt to understand the Bible, and these are the terms on which we turn now to involve ourselves in the Biblical story and see what it will say to us.

CHAPTER

4

The Words of Man and the Word of God

(*The Covenant-Bond*)

Every age of man has contributed its wonders to history. Before the Pyramid of Cheops in the ancient world, the cathedral of Chartres in the medieval world, and the marvel of nuclear fission in the modern scientific world, we must pause and reflect. We cannot escape being impressed as we survey the architectural, the artistic, and the technical achievements of man. If we pause to compare pyramids, Chartres, and $E = MC^2$ with the Bible, we may feel that the Bible really doesn't qualify as one of the wonders of the world. For although it contains some magnificent poetry and some exciting tales, in the last analysis it is only a collection of words. Why, then, did God choose to communicate himself through something that seems, in comparison, to be so inconsequential?

The Supreme Importance of Words

With full appreciation for all the wonders of the world, we must hold nevertheless that God and man can be related *only* through words. Man, in his deepest and most provocative sense, is not a " thing " to be moved hither and yon by im-

42

personal natural forces. A human being can be moved only through *understanding,* and a man or a woman can comprehend only if words are used whose meaning meets response within his or her own mind and heart. If the communication between God and man is to be personal, it must be through the medium, not of things, but of words.

Through words, isolation is banished. A man lost in the Antarctic establishes " radio contact " with his base and is no longer alone. Through words, community is established. Men discuss their common problems and the " town meeting " comes into being. Through words, the scars of loneliness are erased. A person feels cut off from his friends, and then a letter or a phone call or a visit restores his sense of " belonging." Through words, we are " baptized " as communal beings.

So much is true on the human level. How, then, are God and man related? They are not related chemically or biologically or molecularly. They are related through speech! The study of the relationship between God and man is thus called "theology," which means quite literally " God's word." The theology of the Bible declares that God's word has penetrated through our zone of silence, that receiving this word we are enriched, that hearing it our sensitivities are increased, our wisdom and courage magnified. We believe that the wider and the more universal a man's communication the richer his inheritance. Just as a child first receives the speech of his family, is shy with strangers and gradually learns to accept the strangers, so man must constantly increase the range of those with whom he converses. The wider the circle the surer we can be that roughness and narrowness of spirit will be overcome. At the farthest, most universal edge of that circle, a man can, if he listens with humility, hear that voice which is the source of all voices, the *word* of God.

How is the Bible related to all of this? The Bible represents the collective attempt on the part of Hebrew man *to find the words with which God's word can be recorded.* As such, it takes with utmost seriousness the fact that God and man can and do communicate, that they are not silent " at each other." The Bible furthermore recognizes that communication is never easy, that it is never self-evident, that truly personal conversation cannot take place by chattering! And although man, being man, must first understand before he can speak, nevertheless the Bible takes for granted that a relationship has been established, that whether we remember it or not, an introduction has been made. No matter how tongue-tied we may be as individuals, we believe that God has spoken to our fathers, to Abraham, Isaac, and Jacob. The Bible is the account of this ongoing conversation.

The chief characteristic of the word or the words that God spoke to man is that, having been spoken, *they cannot be ignored.* This is the nature of all words. They irrevocably affect the relationship between the speaker and the hearer. Even the word "hello" changes absolutely and unmistakably the relationship between strangers. So do the words, "We're from police headquarters and we'd like to ask you a few questions," or the words, "I love you," or the words, "Get out of this house and out of my life forever." Once any word has been said, whether it is a good word or an evil one, it cannot be retracted, and the word becomes a part of the relationship. A word spoken in hate cannot be retrieved. If the words, "Go to hell!" have been spoken *in hatred,* the inner life of both the speaker and the hearer have been changed. The speaker feels guilty, and the hearer feels fear. Almost any word therefore is fateful, because it takes two beings out of their isolation, out of their unrelatedness and neutrality, and, for good or evil, they become involved with each other.

Once words have been exchanged, the relationship is no

longer potential. A girl may hope that a boy will speak to her. As long as she has only her hopes she has nothing to go on. She can dream freely and without being hindered by reality. She can imagine him saying anything she wants to hear. Once the boy has spoken, however, a relationship emerges and the words constitute a new kind of involvement.

In somewhat the same way Christianity holds that man is related to God concretely. We humans are not in the situation in which we merely hope that God will break his silence. We are convinced that God has spoken and that the concrete character of his speech does give us something to count on. In short, God's speech is not a future possibility but a present reality. We are no longer entitled to daydream about what he *might* say. On the contrary, we have to take seriously what he *has said,* for we know that his speech, his words, have eternal significance for us. The exploration of God's fateful word and the form that it took is precisely the problem that concerns any serious study of the Bible.

A Word Mutually Pledged

Let us now examine quite specifically the way in which this word from God comes to man in the Old Testament. We have seen earlier that God and man share words together. As the Old Testament sees it, these words are not just any casual words. God and man do not merely exchange a quick hello, nod, and go in opposite directions. Nor, in spite of the way we sometimes feel, does God say: " I'm from police headquarters. I'd like to ask you a few questions." No, when the silence is broken, quite a different word emerges, a word arising out of God's deep concern, a word demanding man's complete response.

What, we may well ask, is this strange word? It is not a

question easy to answer since the meaning of that word is
what the whole Bible is about. Nevertheless, we must, even in
this short space, attempt a definition of this special word. Definitions that have been used to suggest the unique meaning of
the word are " contract," " agreement," or " covenant." Each
of these definitions suggests that the word that God and man
hold together is a binding word, a word that suggests a continuous relationship. The phrase that perhaps comes closest to
the original meaning is *covenant-bond*. The covenant-bond is
an agreement that constitutes a pledge. When a man gives his
word, that word, if it is any good, is a binding word, binding
even after the sound of it has passed.

The writers of the Bible were perfectly willing to think of
God and man's relationship in these somewhat human terms.
They were able to do so because, for the prophets, the *pledged
word* was the most responsible and personal relationship that
could be conceived. They knew, however, that the fact that the
covenant-bond was between God and man added a new and
terrible dimension to the relationship. Now, between God and
man, the word pledged was no longer for a month, for ninety
days, or even for a year: it was forever.

We sometimes say that " a man is as good as his word." The
prophets hoped that this would be true of man in his relationship to God. They were not afraid, at the same time, to think
of God as bound by his pledged word. They were convinced
that God's promises were true, that he was " as good as his
word." Indeed, the central theme of the Bible is that man's
true hope rests in the integrity of the divine word.

In so far as God and man are understood as persons, their
relationship is always a pledged word, a covenant-bond. Only
through that covenant-bond are they related at all. They do
not have a mechanical relationship. Man is not a puppet. Only
the word can sustain their relationship. If the covenant-bond

is broken, the relationship is broken. If the pledged words turn out to be worthless, then God and man have nothing in common. The integrity of the word, the covenant-bond, is everything.

What Is Required of Man?

So there is a covenant-bond. What about it? What within this bond do the participants (God and man) do for or about each other? From the point of view of the Bible, what man does for God is to — believe him. Man's task is to believe God, to have faith that he will keep his word, that he will be — God forever.

What, in the covenant-bond, is required of man? To answer this question we must first understand something very important about how the Bible looks at man. The Bible makes clear that what a man *does* comes out of what he *is,* rather than the other way around. It is impossible according to this view to change a man by changing his externals. It is in the interior of the will and mind and heart that one finds the springs of healthy or unhealthy behavior. Obedience follows from faith just as disobedience succeeds unfaith. So, when God commissions Moses to go back from Egypt to free the slaves, the problem becomes one of belief.

Moses, arguing against his commission, says, " But behold, they will not believe me or listen to my voice, for they will say, ' The Lord did not appear to you.' " Moses states the problem clearly. There is no doubt that the " slaves " could organize and escape. They have the physical power to move if only their " belief " can be triggered. Thus does outer behavior always depend upon our interior " attitude." So, if you are unable really to love your neighbor, it will not be long before you will have to force yourself (sometimes with clenched teeth) to do the decent thing for your neighbor. On the other hand, if you are able to love your neighbor, there are no limits to what you will do for him.

In love you can do anything. When love is gone, however, life is chancier and more rules are needed. In the same sense the Bible sees sin to consist of, not disobedience (that can be handled in any true relationship), but unfaith or infidelity. The great demand that the prophets made upon their kings was, therefore, not conformity to God's will, but faith. Thus Isaiah says to Ahaz, a king whose loyalty was thin, who was willing to have an " affair " with another god,

> " If you will not believe,
>   surely you shall not be established " (Isa. 7:9).

It is required of Ahaz, if he is to be in a covenant relationship with God, that he shall believe, against great odds perhaps, that the nation is more secure under God than under its own power. So faith, or believing, is what constitutes man's contribution to the relationship.

The covenant-bond requires that man believe that God is his God forever, and that life will be lived out in joy or despair, in sorrow or fulfillment, but never in a vacuum.

To have faith takes faith. There is no other way of putting it. A husband can love a wife only by loving her. He cannot " work up " to love by counting her good qualities and seeing that they outweigh the bad qualities. When a man loves his wife the good qualities are irrelevant. If, God help him, he cannot love his wife, then an infinity of good qualities will not help. So, too, with faith. One either believes in the integrity of one's partner, one's father, or one's God, or one stands without faith, outside of a covenant-bond.

Such a faith, such a covenant-bond, cannot be maintained as a " doctrine," an abstract rule covering the human race. It is rather the personal risk that each man must take for himself. It is a supreme act of confidence that behind apparent meaninglessness there is always meaning and that behind seeming chaos there is always purpose. By faith, against all odds (and they may be terrible odds), we assert that tomorrow belongs to God. By faith, against the hazards of guilt and fear, we affirm: "And the Lord brought us out of Egypt with a mighty hand and an outstretched arm, with great terror, with signs and wonders; and he brought us into this place and gave us this land, a land flowing with milk and honey." (Deut. 26:8-9.) As long as we believe, we have maintained our betrothal, our covenant-bond with God.

What Is Required of God?

But what of God? What is his obligation? What is required of him in maintaining the covenant? This is more difficult to say. God seems to get off much easier. God has only to be himself. At the same time the Bible does not draw back from asserting that God has a responsibility, and it would seem that God's responsibility is the same as man's — to keep faith. "Know therefore that the Lord your God is God, the faithful God who keeps covenant and steadfast love. . . ." (Deut. 7:9.) God is faithful. This is perhaps the central affirmation of the Bible. His word is good. And what is that word? It is the promise that *God, regardless of man's trustworthiness or lack of it, will stand by — in forgiveness and mercy.*

> "How can I give you up, O Ephraim!
> How can I hand you over, O Israel! . . .
> My heart recoils within me,
> my compassion grows warm and tender.

> I will not execute my fierce anger,
>   I will not again destroy Ephraim;
> for I am God and not man." (Hos. 11:8-9.)

God is faithful. He, God (ridiculous, isn't it?) believes in man! In spite of Sodom and Gomorrah, Buchenwald and Little Rock, Hitler and Stalin, you and me, God is not dissuaded. In spite of our breach of faith, in spite of the fact that we are afraid to trust, he guides us to that Kingdom of which he says: " I will abolish the bow, the sword, and war from the land; and I will make you lie down in safety. And I will betroth you to me for ever; I will betroth you to me in righteousness and in justice, in steadfast love, and in mercy." (Hos. 2:18-20.)

But what does this kind of talk mean today? It means just this. As you look out at all the malignant injustice of the world and as you look inward (far worse) at your own lack of integrity, remember that there is One above whose word is good and who believes in you. If you can respond to that, if you can walk in trust, then like Abraham and Moses you will know the integrity of the covenant-bond.

The Helpless Are Befriended

When did this covenant-bond take place? It took place long ago and it takes place today. When? Originally it took place with Abraham, Isaac, and Jacob; it is renewed with us today. We cannot talk about it without talking about us. We cannot talk about us without talking about it.

Something happened then and something is going on now. We, it will be remembered, believe not merely that God exists but that he " broke silence " as he pledged his word. The word that he pledged to Abraham, Isaac, and Jacob (and to Moses) is the word, the same word that he gives us today. In the covenant-bond, then, there are really three participants: Abraham, God, and you.

Who is Abraham? " Abraham " is actually a name that must be put in quotation marks. We cannot be sure of his identity. He is a symbol for the first of our ancestors who dared to believe that God was reliable, that His word was good.

Somewhere, somewhere in Palestine, several hundred years before David, there were shepherds who were amazed to find their anxieties halted, their fears neutralized. Suddenly the terror of living diminished, the aimlessness of life was overcome as the shepherds became persuaded that their lives were being governed. This group of wanderers, flea-bitten and bedraggled, were convinced that they, against all odds, had a future, that they would have a homeland. A later writer put it into these words for the original nomads when he said, " I am the Lord, the God of Abraham your father and the God of Isaac; the land on which you lie I will give to you and to your descendants; and your descendants shall be like the dust of the earth." (Gen. 28:13-14.)

When, then, did the covenant-bond take place? Let us be honest and acknowledge that we can never be certain of the precise moment when " Abraham " first responded to God's promise. When we come to Moses we still find — uncertainty. Indeed, it is this uncertainty that seems to be one of the elements of the mystery. Even in the account of the covenant-bond with Moses the reader is warned not to " peek through a keyhole " at God. When Moses approaches the burning bush he is told, " Do not come near; put off your shoes from your feet, for the place on which you are standing is holy ground." (Ex. 3:5.)

This is precisely the situation in which we find ourselves as we attempt to understand the original event. The ground which *we* approach is holy ground. We cannot approach that time and place as tourists or even as professional photographers with cameras cocked to capture the first picture of God and Moses. We cannot approach with press card and tape recorder. This "event" cannot be measured by historians, archaeologists, researchers, or reporters. God protects his mystery, wards off all curiosity-seekers who want to confine God to their own understanding of him, and insists that, like Moses, we approach the event — in faith.

So we shall never know the precise moment and the exact conditions of the covenant event. We can be thankful, for thereby is the majesty of God preserved. What we can know is that the earliest writers, writing sometime shortly after King David, sought to describe an event that they could never quite pinpoint. More and more Moses becomes the symbol that gathers up all the ancient faith. All the early writers point again and again to the period of the exodus as the formative period, the period when a group of wandering tribes were fashioned into a unity, a unity that was grounded in a covenant-bond with God.

We will always be a little frustrated when we think of "Abraham" and "Moses." That frustration, however, is meaningful, for it signals to us the fact that we cannot be parasites on the faith of our fathers.

The uncertainty about the precise moment of the *then* forces us to think about the *now*. We too are involved and we cannot understand Abraham's relationship to God apart from our own covenant-bond. We are not onlookers; we are, each one of us, "Abraham" in miniature. And we are not allowed to forget the fact. Thus the later writer of Deuteronomy, speaking to his own age (621 B.C.), reminds the people of every age that they too must respond. "Not with our fathers did the Lord make this covenant, but with us, who are all of us here alive this day." (Deut. 5:3.)

All that we know and all that we need to know is that God chose, in his wisdom and compassion, to relate himself to Israel as that people stood hesitantly between slavery and fulfillment. And we believe that God's word, his invitation to a bonded union, gave a bewildered people the courage to believe and trust that their future would be realized. Trusting in that word, entering into that covenant, they believed and forsook the securities of slavery: they left Egypt and, in faith, went into insecurity. Having done this, they demonstrated for every succeeding generation that God's communication can be grasped only by those who are willing to pass into the wilderness.

The helpless slaves succeed in escaping the formidable army of the Egyptian prince. Life seemed to have a little more justice. When the weak cease to be bullied by the strong, we can almost believe that an Advocate of righteousness has appeared. Into a disordered world a new Champion has come with the assurance that the weak and the helpless shall no longer stand alone. And because of the bond, men no longer in despair, no longer betrayed by their own weakness, can say:

> "If it had not been the Lord who was on our side,
>   when men rose up against us,
>   then they would have swallowed us up alive,
>   when their anger was kindled against us;
>   then the flood would have swept us away,
>   the torrent would have gone over us;
>   then over us would have gone
>   the raging waters.
>
> "Blessed be the Lord,
>   who has not given us
>   as prey to their teeth!

> We have escaped as a bird
>   from the snare of the fowlers;
> the snare is broken,
>   and we have escaped!
>
> " Our help is in the name of the Lord,
>   who made heaven and earth." (Ps. 124:2-8.)

The word that man and God have spoken, the covenant made
between them, is the assurance that history has ceased to be a
no man's land.

AN ANCIENT STORY WHICH IS OUR STORY

We have looked at the covenant-bond as the basis from which we must proceed in " understanding the Bible." We have given it some content, but we must now try to give it more content by looking at other things that happened to the " covenant people " and other things they wrote about. In the process we will begin to see more clearly what we began to see in the last chapter — that " their " story is also " our " story.

Let us start with the early Bible stories. We now know that the stories of the covenant (in the books of Genesis, Exodus, etc.) were not actually recorded at the time when God made the covenant-bond with Israel. Most scholars think of these early records as attempts made by a significantly later generation to understand the mystery of Israel's existence, to seek answers to such questions as: *From whence did we come? How, in the face of so many obstacles, did we make it?*

Such questions as these helped the post-Davidic writers to organize and unify the stories of Abraham, Joseph, and Moses. The fact that the stories were written later does not mean that they were invented. What it means, rather, is that the later writers needed to use all the imagination and intellectual power of maturity in order to indicate something of the majesty of the original event. The nomads simply did not have the experience necessary to write with this kind of imagination.

Being Mature About Maturity

We can, perhaps, understand this " discrepancy " in time between the event and the recording of that event by an analogy within human experience. In the sacrament of Baptism, God makes a covenant with an infant. That covenant is real and binding even though the infant does not have the language or the understanding to express his own participation in the event. The baptized child must go to school, learn language, and mature intellectually and spiritually before he can even grapple with the meaning of what happened to him when he was so helpless. The Hebrew writers themselves were aware of the fact that this is precisely what happened to the infant people: God called them when they were helpless.

" When Israel was a child, I loved him,
    and out of Egypt I called my son. . . .

. . . it was I who taught Ephraim to walk,
    I took them up in my arms;
    but they did not know that I healed them." (Hos. 11:1, 3.)

The ancient Hebrew literature, the Bible, was an attempt to understand an early event so gigantic that it was practically inconceivable. *From whence came we?* and *Who made us?* are questions so profound and so ultimate that they almost defeat the human imagination. Thus, one of the later writers puts on the lips of Moses the feeling of inadequacy that he as a writer must have had when he tried to " explain " how it all started.

"'Oh, my Lord, I am not eloquent, either heretofore or since thou hast spoken to thy servant; but I am slow of speech and of tongue.' Then the Lord said to him, 'Who has made man's mouth? Who makes him dumb, or deaf, or seeing, or blind? Is it not I, the Lord? Now therefore go, and I will be with your mouth and teach you what you shall speak.' But . . . [Moses] said, 'Oh, my Lord, send, I pray, some other person.'" (Ex. 4:10-13.)

The Bible was written by men who were aware of their lack of eloquence. The problems of describing the covenant-bond were such that many could hope with Moses that the Lord might send "some other person." Nevertheless, these later writers did struggle to find the language to speak of God's primary revelation.

It was not until after the exodus from Egypt and after the successful conquest of Palestine (Canaan) that the Hebrews were able to create literature. Under David and Solomon these primitive people matured rapidly. In little more than a generation they moved from tents into houses, from tribal chaos into a centralized state. Furthermore, they developed the military skills necessary to maintain their security against invaders. Rapidly they developed the techniques to build and to organize themselves commercially. Young men, seeing the growing power of their nation, counting their chariots, could look with contempt on the primitive world of their grandfathers. They had every reason to feel comfortable.

Not Everyone Felt Comfortable

Although almost everyone was cheerful and optimistic with the new prosperity of Solomon, a few felt troubled. Probably they did not, at first, know exactly why they were troubled.

As one of the writers thought about the massive palaces and
the proud arches of Solomon's building program, he remembered an ancient nomad tale that also told of how men had
builded, proudly: "Come, let us build ourselves a city, and a
tower with its top in the heavens, and let us make a name for
ourselves. . . . So the Lord scattered them abroad. . . . Therefore its name was called Babel . . ." (Gen. 11:4, 8-9), and
two things seemed to make him afraid:

1. Solomon, in order to achieve his building program, was
violating the ancient tribal concept of brotherhood. Solomon
found it necessary to raise "a levy of *forced* labor out of all
Israel." Thousands were made to work, against their will, in
the forests and the dreaded stone quarries. (I Kings 5:13-18.)
The few whose consciences were disturbed were not inclined
to think that magnificent buildings and national prestige were
worth the enslavement of a portion of the population.

2. The writer (scholars identify him by the letter "J")
was equally disturbed because he saw that national power and
prestige were slowly becoming substitutes for God. "J" may
have been present when Solomon's son, Rehoboam, illustrated
the proud assurance of the regime by saying, "My father made
your yoke heavy, but I will add to your yoke; my father chas-
tised you with whips, but I will chastise you with scorpions."
(I Kings 12:14.)

As "J" struggled and worried he saw a radical contrast
between the claims of this new state and the true power of
Him who had first called Israel from slavery. And, keeping
in mind the utter contrast between Solomon's kingdom and
the true community of God, he created the first Biblical epic.

He began, not with Solomon's puny creations, but with
Him who, without benefit of the artificial power of slavery,
"formed man of dust from the ground, and breathed into his
nostrils the breath of life" (Gen. 2:7). He told of man's ex-

pulsion from Paradise because of his ambition (watch it, Solomon!). He told of two communities in history, the community that lived by faith (Abel, Seth, Abraham) and the community that lived for power (Cain, Enoch, and the builders of Babel, and whoever thereafter lived by *that* code). Some of his readers, at least, during the reign of Solomon or Rehoboam, could not have misunderstood him when he told the story of Abraham trying to save Sodom and Gomorrah (Gen., chs. 18; 19). Sodom, in spite of Abraham's pleas, was destroyed because in it were not to be found as few as ten righteous men!

It was in the exodus, however, that "J" saw the true center of Hebrew history. Indeed, almost all the early writers, during the time of Solomon and after, were fascinated by that moment of mystery, by that hour when God so graciously became the champion of a powerless group of slaves and enabled them to cast off the bonds of a powerful Egyptian king. Later Israel might flex its muscles and imagine that it had lived by its military and economic power, but "J" knew better. There were always some who would not believe in the shekel (the Israelite equivalent of "the almighty dollar"), in chariots, commerce, or kings.

Thus, the faith of the earliest creed: "And you shall make response before the Lord your God, ' A wandering Aramean was my father; and he went down into Egypt and sojourned there, few in number; and there he became a nation, great, mighty, and populous. And the Egyptians treated us harshly, and afflicted us, and laid upon us hard bondage. Then we cried to the Lord the God of our fathers, and the Lord heard our voice, and saw our affliction, our toil, and our oppression; and the Lord brought us out of Egypt with a mighty hand and an outstretched arm, with great terror, with signs and wonders.' " (Deut. 26:5-8.)

Here, in this confession, was the constant reminder that there was One who was greater even than Solomon. Here the child of faith was reminded of Him who had created Israel and called it to freedom.

Freedom or Slavery: A Hard Choice

No matter how much the young nation under Solomon enjoyed feeling secure, there continued to be a few thinkers and writers who were tormented by the memory of that Lord who "brought us into this place and gave us this land, a land flowing with milk and honey." These prophetic writers kept reminding the people that they were not supposed to be the worshipers of a king or a civilization, that they were not supposed to be secure, and that they had been called to freedom. As one of these writers, probably "J," meditated upon the community of faith and freedom (which he hoped to see emerge in the future), he could not help being alarmed by the denial of freedom in a community that concerned itself primarily with security and power. Who, among those who were not being sent to the quarries, cared about freedom anyhow?

And so "J" told the story of the exodus from slavery, of slaves who choose freedom. As "J" saw how easily freedom was lost in his own time he saw that the flight from Egypt, the story that the nomads had told, was really the charter of all human integrity. Through the eyes of "J" and all who were uneasy about Solomonic security (or intercontinental ballistic missiles) we see the drama emerge in which God casts his lot with — freedom. So, filtered through a thousand tellings, the story was finally recorded.

"Then the Lord said, 'I have seen the affliction of my people who are in Egypt, and have heard their cry because of their taskmasters; I know their sufferings, and I have come down to deliver them.'" (Ex. 3:7-8.)

Many a slave must have asked himself as he looked out into the barren wilderness, "Is this trip necessary?" Was freedom worth the risk? Could this fantastic story of Moses be believed? Would it not be better to play it safe? Life was not all that it might be in Egypt, but a man knew what he had, and if one left, conditions might be a great deal worse.

These questions are the inescapable questions that every man must ask as he gauges the risk of his decision. We can understand the anxiety of Israel as it faced the frontier because we, also, can remember our own transitions from helplessness to freedom, our movement from adolescence to maturity. Although some of us may remember happier childhoods than the one Israel called to mind, all of us will recall that, as children, our freedom was radically curtailed by our parents. Most of us also remember that our movement into responsibility was not always made easy by the solicitous concern of our parents. This advance into freedom, we discovered, is always fraught with danger, both from within and from without. Life begins in the womb. There, without any activity on our part, all our wants are satisfied. We are sustained and fed without any effort on our part.

Life always begins in depending upon others. Both children and young nations need the support of an authority in order to be provided with sufficient security so that they, too, can learn to grow into responsibility. Thus, we can see that the modern India is a nation that grew into political maturity because it existed within the structure of the British Empire. We can see, too, that at the right time India demanded its freedom, and by the grace of God, England was able to grant it. For if the freedom is unduly postponed, maturity is itself threatened.

A child who remains under the authority of its parents too long will not risk the responsibilities of freedom. A nation that remains too long in dependency upon a stronger nation soon develops the listlessness of a slave mentality.

The Hebrew slaves, therefore, were not allowed to remain as children. The covenant-bond issues in a task. Israel is sent across the frontier. When the slaves were sent across the frontier, slavery itself came under condemnation. To be free, or to be a slave, was no longer a matter of personal preference. The heart and mind of the universe, the living God, had now committed himself for freedom. Forbidden to remain a slave, Israel was precipitated into the wilderness — there to live or die in freedom.

The story of the exodus is a literary microcosm. That is to say, it makes clear to us that what happens to Israel happens to every man. When God's word meets our mind, when a covenant is made between us, we too are torn out of our securities and thrust into the — unknown! Gone are the safe walls of the city, gone are the securities that the uncovenanted man pursues.

We are, like the Hebrews, most human when we make decisions and act responsibly. It is, however, decisions that are most difficult to make. Sometimes we are fatigued by the number of decisions that we must make. Sometimes we grow anxious because of the uncertainties involved in the decisions that we must make. There is something in the nature of decision itself, if we reflect, that causes us to tremble. We, by the very nature of decision, are asked to assume a responsibility greater than both our strength and our wisdom. When we are too young to know, life asks us to make decisions about our vocation. Many of us would like to have had more time. Perhaps we would have liked an infinite amount of time so that we need not have decided in this life. But He who has made likeness. It involves a willingness to live day by day instead of insisting upon a guaranteed living. It involves freedom in so far as the individual is forced to live in creaturely dependency upon the promises of God, rather than in dependency upon full barns and overflowing vaults.

Creatureliness is a dynamic act of personal living: it is not a static state of existence. This means that, from the point of the Biblical faith, stones and cabbages are not creatures, because both are unresponsive. Each member of the vegetable and mineral kingdoms is what it *is,* for it can be nothing else. Man, however, is a creature. Unlike a stone he is capable of change. He can, by living in trust and love, *become* a person. It is also possible that, once having become a person, he can renounce love, lose everything, and become an animal or a thing.

We read from time to time of hermits, individuals who retreat from society, hole up in some cave and attempt to live in safety, not threatened by love or freedom. Such a man lives, if we can call it living, without being involved in the risks of community existence. He enters into his room and locks the door against the world and freedom. In his world, as much as he can control it, there is security. There are no other voices. Only his animal thoughts keep him alive. He, in this condition, is not a person. He has chosen to be a nonperson, an animal wearing clothes.

We need not, however, look for bizarre illustrations. The flight from creatureliness and the refusal to trust (and the two are synonymous), are acts that occur in our everyday world.

The flight from creatureliness was not unique to the Hebrews. We illustrate it in every act in which we move from our security into the unknown. For many, the "wilderness" that requires the most faith is marriage. There are those who, like the Hebrews, look upon this new relationship as merely an exciting adventure. Such a man looks upon marriage perhaps

us does not allow us to remain children. He has so constructed our life that decisions are unavoidable. All of us have, or will have, fallen in love and each of us must decide whether the love is true or not. Every decision that we make is pregnant with meaning. The very necessity of assuming responsibility unnerves us. We approach the decision and retreat and approach and retreat yet again. From whence shall we derive the strength to quiet our quaking spirits? How can we be sure that this terrible freedom is meaningful, that it is supported by something more than chance, that there is a Universal Love and a Cosmic Concern undergirding those decisions in which every man must live or die? The only answer that we have is the answer given by the prophet.

" Then you shall say to your son, ' We were Pharaoh's slaves in Egypt; and the Lord brought us out of Egypt with a mighty hand; and the Lord showed signs and wonders, great and grievous, against Egypt and against Pharaoh and all his household, before our eyes; and he brought us out from there, that he might bring us in and give us the land which he swore to give to our fathers.'" (Deut. 6:21-23.)

As we know because of the Biblical record, the decision was made and God was trusted and the slaves moved across the swamps and marshes and into the wilderness. Freedom, however, is never won by a single decision. Victory, as Moses discovered, is never automatic.

The Unpleasantness of Second Thoughts — and the Cost of Freedom

Home and hearth and slavery may be stifling, but the wilderness is terrifying. As the Hebrews looked into the grimness of the desert their hope was corrupted by the fact that with every step into the gray unknown they began to regret their decision. With mixed desire they began to think again of the comforts of city and home and womb. As soon as the first step had been taken across the threshold, as soon as danger was felt, Israel cried: "Would that we had died by the hand of the Lord in the land of Egypt, when we sat by the fleshpots and ate bread to the full; for you have brought us out into this wilderness to kill this whole assembly with hunger." (Ex. 16:3.) No sooner does the Hebrew slave taste freedom than he begins to regret his rashness. In the face of bleak sands and confronted by a "Godforsaken" wilderness, the Hebrew begins to question. Human destiny looks like a wild-goose chase. Can anything be believed?

The heart of the man on the threshold of freedom bids him believe "Moses" when he says: "Fear not, stand firm, and see the salvation of the Lord, which he will work for you today; for the Egyptians whom you see today, you shall never see again. The Lord will fight for you, and you have only to be still." (Ex. 14:13-14.)

But it is never easy to be still in the face of danger, and out of the agony of doubt the slave cries: "It would have been better for us to serve the Egyptians than to die in the wilderness." (Ex. 14:12.) To believe or to flee is the issue. How can God be believed when he is masked by a hostile and malevolent world? Who can believe in God when there is no water and no food? Who can see the future shining when the eyes can observe only the darkness? The Hebrew, as he entered the wilderness, was neither slave nor free. He had the loyalty of a slave in the environment of freedom.

This is not simply the problem of the Hebrew, for the Hebrew problem is *the* human problem. For large masses of people in the twentieth century, both fascist and communist

efficiency have appeared to be more attractive than free National security, for both communist and capitalist nat has (as McCarthyism believed) seemed more important integrity of conscience. That *our* world has cast its lot freedom is by no means obvious.

We cannot even be sure that our children really see meaning of freedom. Perhaps this is the nature of freedor that it can never be inherited but each generation must wi all over again. Each individual must seek to cross the fron for himself. That the people of the Bible crossed the fron is no help. Indeed, it is a danger if it tempts us to believe we are free because they were. The fact is that God ensures no one can win freedom for another. *No printed word, word spoken by another, can ever be a substitute for that lon journey each man must make for himself.* There are no prox in the battle for freedom. The only comfort that the young have is that those who risk freedom seem to treasure it much that they have no peace until they have shared it. R turning from danger, they speak with one voice as they assu those who live within the city walls that all the power of t universe seems to undergird man's flight over the drawbridg into freedom.

The Joy and the Risk of Creatureliness

Israel trusted God and crossed the Red Sea into freedom Having entered the wilderness, it looked back at Egypt in stead of up at God and thereby knew *sin*. Unwilling to trust God, insisting upon "security," Israel all but lost its *creatureliness*.

We must examine this further. What is creatureliness? *Creatureliness consists of that quality of life which we have when we trust God.* It is characterized by openness, innocency, child-

hopefully. Entering marriage, he discovers that marriage also involves burdens and responsibilities which he may be unwilling to bear. Thus he hungers for his earlier " bachelor " days. He looks back to his " Egyptian " existence and is unable to accept community living. At best he degenerates into a mere breadwinner. He makes no effort to sustain the imaginative love that characterized his courtship. He takes his relationship to his wife and children for granted. He has thus made a *thing* out of a living relationship, a thing without movement, without color, without spirit, without personal vitality.

Personal existence, in its most risky dimension, is best illustrated in those acts of freedom in which one person either declares his love or friendship for another or on those occasions in which one person asks forgiveness from another. In both cases we always feel an initial fear. It is humiliating to face the possibility of rejection. For some it will be easier, less risky, to avoid the risk of declaring love. In the same fashion it is threatening to one's security to offer an apology, to ask for forgiveness. The other person may not be gracious, may take advantage of one's nakedness and vulnerability. It is easier therefore to risk nothing, to say nothing and — to be nothing.

Nevertheless, because God sent the slaves across the swamp to freedom, those moments in which we remember ourselves to have been most real, most truly personal, are those moments when we revealed our love or our loyalty or our humility. We live dependently, helplessly, as creatures when we cross the frontier and either give or receive forgiveness. When we live faithfully we live as creatures risking everything for truth. When we exist in an uncreaturely manner we risk nothing because we do not open ourselves to danger. We merely possess ourselves in a dull and routine manner.

As we have seen, creatureliness represents a willingness to live in freedom, in risk, in trust. The opposite of creatureliness

is surely sin, where man refuses to be free, where he insists on
" security."

" Secure " Churches Miss the Point

So this ancient tale says a lot to us as individuals. But it says
a lot more too. For if we think of sin in terms of the refusal to
accept creatureliness, the refusal to live in faith instead of in
terms of booze and fornication, then the church is in trouble.
For the church, if we accept a Biblical instead of a puritan con-
ception of sin, has become in our time the most *respectable* of
communities. To the bewilderment of many observers, it has
accomplished this while serving Him who, for our sakes, became an *outcast.*

The church has achieved this conventional position because
it has concerned itself, not with its own precarious relation to
eternity, but with the greater " fun " of attacking the world.
By criticizing the world for its " worldliness," the church has
purchased for itself a cheap immunity. Instead of struggling
with its own guilt and thereby crossing into new frontiers, it
has gone back into Egypt, into a dull security.

The church weakens its unique contribution by associating
sin with " the world." The real difference between the church
and the world is found, rather, in the fact that the *word* has
been spoken to the one and, as yet, not to the other.

The world waits for a word that it has not yet heard. As
such, the world does not really know what sin is. In a certain
sense the world is innocent and, while it can do good or evil,
it cannot sin, cannot break a covenant that in its own life has
not yet been realized. The world is characterized by *receptivity,
incompleteness.*

The church, on the other hand, is characterized by the fact
that it is a witness, that it has received, that it has heard, that

the word is engraved on its memory and literature. The problem of the church is the problem of forgetting, of refusing to remember, freedom, faith, and insecurity. The church is a community that does not dare believe what it has heard. The church, like the Hebrews, hovers between faith and sin. When it chooses to believe its word, it acts in faith. When it will not believe, it acts in sin. Unable to believe, the church forsakes creatureliness and flees into some security structure of its own.

The church constantly finds itself in the situation of protecting itself from its destiny. Like Israel, the church does not dare to believe that it must go into the wilderness. It forsakes the risk of faith and lives by imitating the faith of its fathers. This means that it lives on the strength of a past faith, that it is unwilling to cross the frontier in its own day. The price to be paid for the refusal to go into the wilderness is a loss of vitality. It is for this reason that clergymen feel most secure when they are criticizing either breweries or gambling. On the issues of *our* day — the great questions of the control of atomic resources, the social and economic failures of Christendom — the church is silent. It is precisely in the church's unwillingness to live freely and critically that we see the greatest obstacle for a renewal of the covenant-faith in our day.

Let this be said, then, with all emphasis and all earnestness. And let it be said again and again. But let it not be the last word that is said. For beyond our failure to keep the covenant lies a promise for the renewal of the covenant, and it is this fact that we must now turn to explore.

6

RE-CREATION AND RENEWAL

We have a long path to trace in this chapter, but it is the most important path we can walk. It will take us from ourselves back to the first century, and then bring us back to ourselves again.

In order to become human, we must face our Creator. How? We do not face God in the manner of a policeman staring, with eyes of steel and contempt, at a traffic violator. Nor do we face God triumphantly in the manner of a cat about to pounce upon a helpless mouse. We are neither policemen nor cats. We are *creatures* of God. And as creatures we must face God with all the fear and trembling that belong properly to creaturely existence.

However, as any careful observer of the human situation knows, we are not very accomplished in the art of accepting limitations. The history of our relationship to God is always the history of our refusal to accept the relationship on the terms demanded. Tempted by our freedom, we always become boundary breakers. We are asked to serve God on earth. We prefer to serve God by first putting one foot in heaven. We do not object to the most onerous service so long as it does not involve uncertainty and risk. We will do all that is required as long as we have an iron assurance that we are no longer vulnerable and helpless. We will make the most inspired sacrifices. We will climb the highest mountains and jump the widest crevasses. We will deny earthly rulers and face the most terrible jeopardy. We will, if it is required, even do all these things while assuming the modesty of a saint.

We will be heroes for God . . . but never creatures.

The Strangeness of God

Ancient Greece and Rome had created extraordinarily high religious philosophies. The most dedicated Christian could not hope to exceed the integrity of Socrates or the moral responsibility of Epictetus. No one could surpass these pagans in their sense of high and holy living.

Paganism appealed to each man on the basis of the intelligence that resided within him. The intelligence within each man was assumed to be identical with that larger intelligence which was directing the course of the universe. If a man did not heed this " wisdom," he wasted his life in confusion and error and he made wrong choices; instead of accentuating his mind he emphasized his flesh. But if a man heeded the demands of intelligence, he would dedicate his life toward that which was pure and noble.

The religion of the Bible, by contrast, differed from this " high " view of paganism in two ways. In the first place, the Biblical man was not so sure that the fulfillment of life came from going " higher." He rather thought that our life on earth was good, that it had to be fulfilled in the here and now. Thus Jesus says,

> " Thy kingdom come,
>   Thy will be done,
>   On earth as it is in heaven." (Matt. 6:10.)

In the second place, the Biblical man differed from the pagan man in that he could not bring himself to believe that either his intelligence or his spirit was a trustworthy road to God. Indeed, he found it slightly inconceivable to believe that God was to be found at the end of a thought:

> "For as the heavens are higher than the earth,
>   so are my ways higher than your ways
>   and my thoughts than your thoughts." (Isa. 55:9.)

God could only be understood as One who was infinitely more than man, a transcendent being with whom man could never feel entirely familiar, a Holy Stranger with whom man could never be comfortable.

So the Hebrew did not attempt to find God through the logic of his mind. Instead, he declared that God was grounded in a mystery that preceded all thought and understanding. God could only be understood as the One who had brought a helpless group of slaves into freedom and purpose. So each Hebrew child was taught, not to think his way up to God, but to remember that "we were Pharaoh's slaves in Egypt; and the Lord brought us out of Egypt with a mighty hand." (Deut. 6:21.)

Christendom has chosen to cast its lot with the faith of that Hebrew child and not with the wisdom of great philosophers. We also are convinced that God is found, not in the mirror of our thoughts and feelings, but in that strange world of Abraham, Isaac, and Jacob. The pagan felt that God was *in continuity* with man. This meant that man could move directly out to the end of his thought and find — God. Although Christianity has a deep appreciation for thinking, it is convinced that God lives *beyond* our thought and feeling and sense.

The Christian discovers that the strangeness of the exodus

event breaks into every intellectual reverie. The covenant event keeps us from getting lost in ourselves, from becoming intoxicated by the potency of our thoughts. There is thus always a tension between thought and the Bible. Whenever we think, we find the Bible irritating. Abraham, Moses, and an obscure Semitic people interrupt our love affair with ourselves. We are drawn to One who is infinitely more than we are, before whom our thoughts are only broken bridges. We are filled with foreboding. Although, with the Greek philosophers, we feel intellectually confident before nature and logic, we feel different when we try to " think " our way to God. Before him we feel fragile and uncertain. Before him our logic collapses and, with Francis Thompson, we confess:

> " I fled Him, down the nights and down the days;
>   I fled Him, down the arches of the years;
> I fled Him, down the labyrinthine ways
>   Of my own mind; and in the mist of tears
> I hid from Him, and under running laughter.
>   Up vistaed hopes I sped;
>   And shot, precipitated,
> Adown Titantic glooms of chasmed fears,
>   From those strong Feet that followed, followed after."

Faith Struggles with Evasions

This is unpleasant. For as soon as God becomes more than our thoughts we become uncomfortable. We begin to wonder whether there is any alternative to the uncertainty that comes from the sounds of " those strong Feet that followed, followed after."

The early Christians discovered that there *was* an alternative to the Holy Stranger from whom men fled " down the arches

of the years." The religion of the New Testament provided
them with a happier possibility. If man was a little uneasy in
the presence of the Creator, he could find warmth and understanding in Jesus. Cheerfully he substituted the familiar voice
of Jesus for the uncertain voice of the Holy Stranger. He
learned to forget the sound of those Feet following after as he
listened to Him who said:

" Come to me, all who labor and are heavy-laden, and I will
give you rest. Take my yoke upon you, and learn from me;
for I am gentle and lowly in heart, and you will find rest for
your souls. For my yoke is easy, and my burden is light."
(Matt. 11:28-30.)

Many of the best minds of the second century came to the
conclusion that it was possible to build a religion without fear,
a religion without strangeness, a religion in which man could
be at home with God.

If the reader of *this* volume has found that the last paragraph
sounds more persuasive than has the heavy burden of " creatureliness," he may derive such comfort as he is able from the
fact that he has repeated the earliest, the most original, and
the most persistent, of the heresies that have ever afflicted the
Christian faith.

There were many different heretics in the early church. They
all had one idea in common, a suspicion that the world above
and the world below could not be related. Most heretics were
world-weary. As a result of this " fatigue " the heretic drove a
wedge between Jesus and God, between redemption and creation. How could the Lord who had made this " nasty " world
have anything to do with the Jesus who, it was believed, was
trying to save us from this impure world?

The heresies, having their roots in the high hopes of paganism, found the Christian notion of *lowliness* particularly unacceptable. How, from the point of view of any pure ideas, could anyone ever imagine that the *womb* should be holy, that *food* should have sacramental significance, and, above all, that the Divine should descend lower and lower until he was born in a *stable?*

While the pagan thinkers were "looking upward," Christians were concerning themselves with Him who *lowered* himself.

"Have this mind among yourselves, which you have in Christ Jesus, who, though he was in the form of God, did not count equality with God a thing to be grasped, but emptied himself, taking the form of a servant, being born in the likeness of men." (Phil. 2:5-7.)

What was even worse was the fact that the followers of Jesus seemed to admire his *lowliness* (rather than *continuity* with God). Instead of aiming for heroic achievements, the Christian believed that life would be fulfilled by serving the sick, the poor, and the Godforsaken. Christians did not have even minimal standards of decency. The pagan religious schools limited themselves to members who at least tried to live nobly; Christians, however, would accept *anybody*. So one of the noblest of the pagans, Celsus, spoke in mockery: "Let us hear whom they invite: whoever is a sinner, whosoever is without understanding, whoever is foolish, in fact, whoever is unfortunate, him will the Kingdom of God receive."

It was Paul who saw that that weakness which the pagans rejected was the ground of the Christians' humility. "God chose what is low and despised in the world, even things that are not, to bring to nothing things that are, so that no human being might boast in the presence of God." (I Cor. 1:28-29.)

Christianity, under attack, built its defenses in terms of both Bible and creeds.

First, let us look at the issue of the Bible. In the second century, Christians had no Bible, properly speaking. Since the majority of Christians were now Gentiles rather than Jews, it was not clear that the church should still hold to the Hebrew Scriptures (our present Old Testament). Furthermore, the resurrection faith had provided a number of gospels and letters, but these were scattered in various churches. Slowly a group of the gospels and some of the letters were accepted by many of the leading churches. But what about those ancient Hebrew Scriptures? Should they also be classed as authoritative literature?

The heretics said no. They held that the God of the Hebrew Scriptures did not measure up to the divinity within Jesus Christ. The God of the Old Testament was a God strangely mixed up with *things*. Whoever has not, at some time or another, despaired of the *things* of this world? Those who have wanted to flee from a world in which there are narcotics, alcohol, or sex, will surely understand the protest of those who defended a "heavenly" religion. Their cry was, *Let us go beyond the earth and we shall be out of the reach of evil.* But the rest of the early Christians saw that faith could not forsake a world that God had stooped to save. The church held fast to the faith that, in Christ, *this* world had been made good.

Heretics attacked the flesh as well as the Creator-God. How could the pure Jesus be made of flesh? If the *real* Jesus had been in a body, he would have been corrupted just like the rest of us. But, countered the church, he had been *seen* and one of the disciples, Thomas, had *touched* him. Nonsense, said the heretics, this was an illusion. Jesus had "used" a body in concession to human weakness, but his body was not at all important to his personality. Being truly divine, he was above hunger and suffering.

Not so, said the church. If Jesus was not human, not in the body of a creature, then we can have no real communion with him. Out of love he *joined* the human race. The church, moreover, did not feel that humanity was an affront to divinity. Thus the great creed of Chalcedon affirmed that the human and the divine could dwell in harmony. Affirming that Jesus was " truly God and truly man," the church declared that God, in Christ, did not find humanity obnoxious.

In the most magnificent of its creeds, the Nicene, the church gave its radical answer to those who depreciated the world and its Creator, as the italicized lines in particular show.

"I believe in one God the Father Almighty, Maker *of heaven and earth,* and of all things visible and invisible;

And in one Lord Jesus Christ, the only-begotten Son of God, begotten of his Father before all worlds; God of God; Light of Light; Very God of Very God; begotten, not made; *being of one substance with the Father,* by whom all things were made; who for us men, and for our salvation, *came down from heaven. . . .*"

Taking this creed seriously, we shall not attempt to escape from God through Jesus. Jesus came to renew the Kingdom *of the Creator,* a world in which true authority is clothed in gentleness, in which meekness walks in strength, a world capable of receiving the Messiah.

The Stumbling Block

Who is Jesus? The answer to this question depends upon where we stand. Living in an age that has boasted of its practicality, we tend to avoid high-sounding ecclesiastical and theological language. We would prefer to think of Jesus as a friend with influence in high places. We see him primarily as a counselor, a friendly guide, through life's complex decisions. No matter how great the crisis — from hangnails to fallen arches — we can always " take it to the Lord in prayer! " Our modern Jesus, perhaps influenced by the soap operas, always has an answer to life's problems. With him we do not need to put on airs. In this view, the Messiah has become so commonplace that he has infinitely less mystery to his personality than any great statesman or, for that matter, any significant dramatic artist. It would never occur to this modern thinker that Jesus could not be " thought." With almost a pagan simplicity he could assume a *continuity* between his own mind and the reality of the Messiah.

But if we turn away from this " easy " view to the New Testament, we will discover that the life and work of Jesus cannot be so easily " gotten into our heads." His enemies complain because he " ate with tax collectors and sinners." He seems to be so strange that, upon hearing him, observers say: " What is this? A new teaching! " (Mark 1:27) or " Who then is this, that even wind and sea obey him? " (Mark 4:41). His disciples are not even sure of his identity. Some of them think that he is John the Baptist. (Mark 8:28.) Others of them, perhaps all, thought that he had come to set up a new empire.

This is not quick familiarity, but rather uneasiness and uncertainty. In the realities of the New Testament, men come face to face with their own inability to understand. Confronted by Jesus, they feel the impossibility of gaining knowledge. Here they stand, in all the awkwardness that superficial religion attempts to hide.

The difference is clear. For the *modern* man, Jesus represents the fulfillment of his hopes. For the *New Testament* man, Jesus represents the abandonment of hope. Thus, whatever had been the expectations of the disciples, when he was arrested they were convinced that he had " betrayed " them, and so, we are told, " they all forsook him, and fled " (Mark 14:50). The New Testament does not disguise the embarrassment that Jesus was to those who should have best known him. Who is he?

" And on the sabbath he began to teach in the synagogue; and many who heard him were astonished, saying, ' Where did this man get all this? What is the wisdom given to him? What mighty works are wrought by his hands! Is not this the carpenter, the son of Mary and brother of James and Joses and Judas and Simon, and are not his sisters here with us? ' *And they took offense at him."* (Mark 6:2-3.)

It was Paul who saw that the " offense " of Jesus, his incomprehensibility, had central theological significance. That the Messiah was an embarrassment was not an accident. The fact that Jesus cannot be understood is not something that we can brush aside. *Our failure to understand is itself part of the intent of revelation.* Thus, most perceptively, does Paul say that " we preach Christ crucified, a stumbling-block to Jews and folly to Gentiles." (I Cor. 1:23.)

Why is Jesus a stumbling block to the understanding? Why is he folly?

It is because he is crucified.

How can God be crucified? How is it possible for the most ultimate of all power to be broken? Why did Jesus fail? Anybody can fail. That is, anybody but God. If it had been claimed that Jesus had been just a courageous *man,* then there would have been no embarrassment. It seems almost to be the lot of a courageous man to drink hemlock or be crucified or go to jail. But how can *God* die? Do we not expect God to come *in power?* How could he who had been victorious over demons and Satan be overcome by a platoon of Roman soldiers? How — if he were truly God?

And it is precisely on this question that the faith of many has collapsed. On the basis of his death and integrity, many can admire him, but to believe in him is quite another matter. Those who, at his death, scoffed and said, " He saved others; let him save himself, if he is the Christ of God, his Chosen One! " (Luke 23:35) were absolutely correct in *their* logic. But (and here Christianity stands or falls) the coming of the Messiah signifies that we must relate ourselves to God on *his* terms and not on our logic. This does not mean that our human logic is not meaningful, but it does mean that the rationality that God gave us as a gift cannot, impregnated by pride, be directed against him. Yet this is what has happened. We have, through thinking, attempted to set limits upon the freedom of God. We decide how He who gave us our understanding must himself be understood. We use our reason as a weapon against God. If, we argue, God exists, then let him prove that existence to us by some demonstration of power. If God exists, we further argue, we have no objection to recognizing him, but we do require that he first set the world aright. If God is righteous, then let him show us a little of that righteousness in our times — then we will be glad to support his claim to the Godhead. A God who acts like God we can understand, but a God who sends his Son to die has proved nothing, has demonstrated only that he is as ineffectual as the rest of us.

Neither the modern man nor the pagan man understood how seriously the problem of pride interfered with man's understanding of God. As a result, neither comprehended the fact that God, in order to be understood, had first to shatter the hardness of human pride. And human pride *was* shattered with unbelievable force when the Messiah came, not as a mighty God but as a broken and crucified figure. It is before that cross and its brokenness that man discovers the need for a similar brokenness within his own heart. It is the absurdity of the cross that reminds man that between him and his Creator a bridge has been washed out, and that before the abyss man can only stand in helplessness.

The Jesus of the New Testament remains an eternal stumbling block. He whom we see to be *the* problem of understanding reminds us of the problem that we are to ourselves. Even though, as Christians, we *believe* him, still faith itself retains some uncertainty. We can never put Jesus on a matter-of-fact basis. He never becomes a piece of the information in our heads. We can memorize a thousand texts and proclaim them with uncreaturely assurance and still Jesus remains unsolved.

If Christ were an easy and natural answer, we could, through him, ease ourselves out of the difficulties that belong to existence and to faith. Instead of agony and sweat, which belong to creaturehood, we could then believe as easily as blinking the eyes or sneezing. Or, to put it in another way, God the Creator has always been a problem for every man. The coming of the Messiah does not make that problem any the less.

God gives man dignity by giving him difficulty. Men deny their creatureliness (and their dignity) when they try to avoid the difficulty. A faith without agony, a knowledge of God without uncertainty, is the coveted goal of the person who refuses to be a creature under God. God underlines his faith in human destiny by coming to man through the frail flesh of Christ. The fact that the mighty God comes in frailty becomes a stumbling block. If he came in strength, we would not be disappointed; but who can believe — a crucified carpenter?

The truth is that we can look at the Messiah only in fear and trembling, only as those in whom belief and unbelief eternally struggle. Jesus meets us just where we are most uncertain. Like the awkward disciples (who were never as sure of themselves as are orthodox Christians) we can never put our best

foot forward. Uncertainty causes us to stumble. And just when
we recover and are about to make a ringing, roof-shattering
declaration of faith, our voices crack and we hear ourselves
whisper, " I believe; help my unbelief! " (Mark 9:24.)

How could we be servants with the Servant-Messiah and live
in the castles of granite orthodoxy? How could we live behind
the battlements of impregnable doctrine and still share with
the Messiah the frailty that marks a Son of God? Of himself,
he said, " Foxes have holes, and birds of the air have nests; but
the Son of man has nowhere to lay his head." (Matt. 8:20.)

Re-creation and Renewal

We have now come to the point where we must ask the question, What is the total aim of the Bible? Where is it leading
us? Let us assume that the reader has accepted the fact that
creatureliness is the condition for understanding. Therefore,
he reads carefully (rather than easily); he tries to understand
what he is reading in relation to the minds of the original authors. He does not attempt to force the Bible to say what he
wants it to say. He abstains, therefore, from superimposing his
logic (or that of the church, for that matter) on what is being
communicated. Finally, he is willing to think in terms of
brokenness (with the New Testament) instead of in terms of
continuity (with paganism). After all this has been accomplished, he has the right to ask the question, What have I
learned? How does the whole enterprise — the sequential voice
of the Bible and the understanding of the reader — come into
clear focus?

The understanding of the reader and the " story " within the
Bible come together at the point where it becomes clear that
the renewal of creation (and the covenant community) is
neither an event that will happen (maybe) in the future, nor

merely a "story," interesting but irrelevant to the real world in which we must live.

The message of the Bible (terribly simplified) is this: Because of something God has done we are now living within a redeemed history. The Kingdom of God is not to be found in daydreaming, nor will it be found in some ever-receding future. The ultimate word of the Biblical faith is this — *all that God has ever promised is now available.* If the Biblical faith is true, the full resource of God's power is *presently* available for the healing of men and of nations.

"What?" the immediate response goes. "How can that be possible? Read the newspapers! Unless the Kingdom of God is fulfilled in threats of war, murder, and embezzlement we have missed its coming." Is there any answer to the charge that contemporary history just doesn't look like the Kingdom of God?

This is a difficult problem, and there are all kinds of ways of cheating. It is possible to argue that the Kingdom of God is available only later — in heaven, or to argue that the power of God is not in a kingdom but in the hearts of individuals. Neither of these answers will do since, if the Kingdom of God is to be in heaven, it just isn't real as far as human beings are concerned. We still live on earth. If that Kingdom, on the other hand, is restricted to the individual, if it is a merely private matter, then it isn't a kingdom and we cannot speak as the Bible does of a covenanted *community*.

What is the answer? Or better, how do we go about finding the answer? We find it only if we remember and take seriously the implications of the stumbling block for our own thinking. Being believers (if we are) does not exempt us from the difficulty that every man must face as he tries to understand God. This is to say that, at every point, we have to decide whether we will think from the standpoint of *continuity* or out of *brokenness.* Continuity, of course, presupposes that understanding is directly possible, and brokenness presumes that understanding is possible only through aid that comes from beyond the seeker.

If we make a serious attempt, we can move back to the more fragile atmosphere of the New Testament world. If we do that, then we begin by affirming the truth, and that is that everything within us protests against comprehending what Jesus meant by the Kingdom of God. In this case we are like the disciples. We suspect what he means, but we know precisely what we want. We want the Kingdom of God *only* if it is in a form that will not imperil any of our holdings. What we really want is a world in which we are important *and* a God who declares that our importance is according to his plan. We want the security of our empire. We are not at all averse to being rich, whether in power or money or prestige or recognition. We just do not happen to like fragility.

We can begin to understand Jesus only by admitting that *we* are politely, but nevertheless unutterably, opposed to the Kingdom of God. It is true, of course, that we are more amenable to talking about it than secular people are, but we also want some fulfillment that we can understand. Perhaps special recognition will be enough, but some special reward for our sacrifices is required. Even a bank gives dividends. Does God do less?

The truth is that we are *offended* at the symbol of the cross. We want to be first — but not first to the cross. The truth is that this is precisely what offends us, the suspicion that maybe after all the cross plays havoc with *our* hopes. And offended, we are at least honest. Offended, we have joined the disciples and recognized that we cannot think ourselves into understanding.

We suspect, as did the disciples, that Jesus calls us, not to fulfillment, but to suffering, that he calls us (dreadful thought) to be inconspicuous in our servanthood, vulnerable in our love, defenseless in our sympathy.

Who, in his right mind, wants that? God insults our hopes. He offers us all the power of the universe so that we can give up our little power. The Kingdom of *God* offends us from first to last. Now if we do not admit that we are offended, we will never understand. If we do not admit the offense, then we have refused to accept the category which the Bible gives us so that we can understand its message. Does a man read German with a French dictionary? Does a man read a mathematical equation with the standards of a historian? Does a student read the Bible with the criterion of paganism?

This power — to lose our fears and to be free — is a possibility that is by no means limited to the interior of individuals. It also affects, in so far as men are willing to receive it, the course of history. It changes the relation of father to son, of a government to its citizens, of a nation toward its enemies. When pride is broken, when men find their freedom, whenever men accept the fact that they are offended, then, and only then, it is possible that nations shall

" beat their swords into plowshares,
and their spears into pruning hooks." (Micah 4:3.)

What does this power (which the Bible calls *grace*) do to human freedom? Does this gift annul our freedom and make us into robots? Many critics and some friends of the Hebrew-Christian tradition have argued that the idea of grace erodes human responsibility. It is possible to get at this view through some ironclad logic (easy views of double predestination, etc.), but if we follow the Biblical account, this is not the case. The Bible assumes that God and man have a relationship in which each of them must contribute: this notion of mutual responsibility is, as was suggested in Chapter 4, the ground of covenant religion. The God who relates himself to man through a *word* does not treat man as though he were a thing. Word and message and book, indeed, involve the opposite of thing; they demand a response and not merely a reaction (as in chemistry).

How can we understand this grace? On one level it is not difficult. On another level it is grounded in offense. On the first level, grace means the power by which a broken relationship is renewed. Paul describes it, therefore, as "peace with God" (Rom. 5:1), "reconciled" to God (v. 11). Now peace and reconciliation we can understand, for these terms represent activities that are going on about us all the time.

We know, all too well, the shock that affects us whenever we experience a broken word. When we count on a person's statement and the promise collapses, then our relation to that person is seriously affected. Indeed, the breaking of a pledged word frequently destroys community. This is most dramatically true in that community which rests upon the promises of marriage. In the creation of this community a man is asked whether he, "*forsaking all others,* [will] keep thee only unto her, so long as ye both shall live." If he so promises, and thereby creates that trust which is the ground of all true community, he cannot break his promise and still have the community. If he breaks his word and does not "forsake all others," he cannot, no matter how hard he tries, have true communion with her to whom he made the promise. He cannot count on the trust and confidence that he was formerly given. Indeed, once his word is broken, the relationship has died. The man who broke the covenant has no power to make the relationship come alive again. He waits helplessly upon his wife. He can hope that she will forgive. He can even promise that he will never again be unfaithful. It does not matter. Only the injured person can, in the mystery of love, declare that the violation is as though it were not. Only she can, through her love, restore an integrity that the husband had easily thrown away. The point is that the one who breaks the covenant is powerless. Only the person who has been injured has the power to forgive. And before that power, whether in God or in our neighbor, we can only wait in hope.

Man *is* helpless before the God whom he has betrayed. He transfers the loyalty that he owes his Creator to the earthly "gods" of national security, racial arrogance, ecclesiastical pride. His relationship to God by any of these acts is broken. In that situation there is nothing that man can do. Desperate promises, earnest excuses, reluctant contrition cannot restore a broken community. Regret cannot re-create trust.

The uncovenanted man, like an adulterer, now literally has no God. His words are addressed to . . . nothing. He listens to . . . silence. He is alone, sustained only by the memory that he once lived, loved, and was trusted.

Only God has the power to renew a broken faith. Only God has the grace to forgive and to restore. And it is this renewal and restoration that the Bible proclaims. By God's mercy we are no longer alone with our cheap gods and silence. By grace we are restored to communion with our Creator.

What the Bible captures so magnificently, in its account of this grace, is the simplicity of the renewal. Man, like a child, discovers the joy of the divine love. God, like a father, renews generously and without hesitation. Nowhere has the grandeur of forgiving love been more dramatically described than in the story of the prodigal son who, returning home to he knows not what, discovers that " while he was yet at a distance, his father saw him and had compassion, and ran and embraced him and kissed him " (Luke 15:20). So does God forgive, so guilt and self-hatred are covered by the new significance that God at-

taches to human life. This forgiveness we can understand for,
being human, we have learned of renewal through our parents
and our friends.

What we find difficult to understand is the *form* in which
that forgiveness was given. In the Bible the signal of that forgiveness is the resurrection of Jesus Christ. Many theologians
have constructed highly rational theories that have explained
the "sense" of the crucifixion and resurrection. Some have
thought that God allowed his Son to be killed as a ransom to
the devil; others have argued that God's honor had been injured and that someone had to pay. None of these theories is
satisfactory, and this volume will not add another awkward
theory to that list.

Christians should, rather, speak with frankness and declare
that a completely satisfactory explanation of the atonement is
impossible. All reasoning breaks down before the deepest mystery of faith. It is at this crucial center that we must be most
convinced of the discontinuity (brokenness) of thought and
reality. The meaning of the resurrection cannot be explained.

Although God's grace in Christ cannot be explained in a
clear and fixed form, some of its meaning can be understood.
If we cannot understand the center of the mystery, we can, at
least, look toward its outer edges. When we look toward those
edges we do recognize that in the life, death, and resurrection
of Jesus, God has concentrated our attention on a figure who is
himself radically different from every other historical figure
and who asks us to live, as he did, in love.

It is God's grace that renews us, that restores us to our lost
humanity. We become human, trusting and hoping, when we
cease trying to live like gods, secure and invulnerable. It is
God who, by his mercy, takes us out of the solitude of our driv-
ing ambition and gives us again our neighbor. For it is the
"broken" Christ who shatters our iron sufficiency, who

" weakens " us and thereby helps us to accept our creaturehood gladly. It is the image of the Suffering Servant who teaches us that we live, not by our clever strengths, but through openness of trust.

" Have this mind among yourselves, which you have in Christ Jesus, who, though he was in the form of God, did not count equality with God a thing to be grasped, but emptied himself, taking the form of a servant, being born in the likeness of men. And being found in human form he humbled himself and became obedient unto death, even death on a cross. Therefore God has highly exalted him and bestowed on him the name which is above every name, that at the name of Jesus every knee should bow, in heaven and on earth and under the earth, and every tongue confess that Jesus Christ is Lord, to the glory of God the Father." (Phil. 2:5-11.)

Epilogue

This introduction to the study of the Bible has been able to discuss only the problems of the two centers of the Biblical literature, the stories of the Creation and of the covenant community and the renewal of the covenant community. The student of the Bible will want, not only to keep these two centers in mind, but also to move out into the other themes important to a community that had rich and diverse interests. The people of the Bible, like ourselves, were interested in a multiplicity of areas. The various men who wrote the Biblical literature were frequently successful in seeing the ultimate foundations of politics, economics, war, and peace. They did not, as they faced these problems, write with a formula, and, as a result, the reader will be intrigued with the genuine diversity of opinion that marked this ancient culture.

Amidst the rich diversity the student will discover that almost every Biblical writer is concerned with the acts of God. Because God is believed to be the source of all goodness and creativity the Biblical writer believed that man was absolutely dependent upon understanding how God was influencing his life. In contrast to many other ancient religions the Biblical writer almost always believed that God was influencing man for good. God was neither indifferent nor malevolent, and although he frequently punished man, his aim was always *the renewal of life*. The whole story of the Bible is, then, the drama by which the reader can become aware of God's promise, His faithfulness under adversity (man's faithlessness), and His ultimate victory.

The Bible, as we can see, is a very important book. It is not, however, the only book in the world, and a childish pride should not make us claim that it is even the most important book in the world. A book is only important in relation to the purpose for which it is being used. An engineer, building a bridge, would find a book of engineering principles more useful. The Bible is not a textbook on medicine or any kind of science, for that matter. It cannot be made into a source for all wisdom, for it is not. It is a book concerned, in its poetry and its stories, with the way in which God seeks man for communion with himself.

The Bible, then, must be seen to be an important book among *other* important books. Christianity, in its weaker moments, has not always admitted that this was the case. Christians, interpreting the Bible, have sometimes felt that the Biblical truth must be superior to any truths that even seem to be different or contradictory. This position is not without some logic. Indeed, from the point of view of the logician, it would be impossible to have two views in contradiction on the same question and to have the possibility of both views being right. Although the Christian respects logic, he recognizes that there is another dimension to truth, the dimension of creatureliness. For wherever faith exists without a corresponding sense of creatureliness the result is arrogance! Wherever faith combines with creatureliness the result is a knowledge grounded in humility. If God came to man not in terrible strength but in gentle weakness and if he came that we, too, might be *lowered,* then we cannot, in faith, make the Bible into a weapon to be used proudly against those whom we may not understand or agree with. It would be easy to take the Bible and use it as a cosmic eraser to eliminate other points of view, as Hinduism or Buddhism. We will be especially humble as we relate ourselves to those with whom we share the covenant — the Jews. The believer who, for Christ's sake, abandons iron logic will discover that he can both believe and still have openness and respect for other positions. It may be uncomfortable, but we must learn to relate our creatureliness to the way in which we look at the Bible. There will be some consolation, however, in discovering that we can move out from the world of the Bible to the world of general culture.

Finally, if we study the Bible carefully, we will discover that, although God has commenced the renewal of humanity, the present order of family and community is not yet the Kingdom of God. As such, the Bible will give little comfort to either the pessimist or the optimist. Against the pessimist the interpreter of the Bible must hold that God, and not the devil, is now at work in our history. Against the optimist it must be said that our history is not yet fulfilled, and that as believers we look toward that day when God's will will be done on earth as it is in heaven.

This means that, if we are to do justice to the complexity of the Bible at this point, we must do two things simultaneously. First, we must be concerned with, and very critical of, the structures of family, economics, and politics. We cannot retreat into our private piety if God is at work in the " outer " world. That world, the world of job and profession, may well be a world which is dominated by the lust for power. But it is also God's world, a world which waits for love and trust. We cannot be satisfied with the world as it is. We must bring to it all the concern and compassion that mark God's involvement with human history.

Secondly, although we must be critical of the world because it is not yet the Kingdom of God, we must not, however, be too critical of it. For our world, with all its flaws, is a world into which God is pouring his faith. It is not an evil world, for whatsoever evil there is has been qualified by Him who came to set our world and our lives free. We must not, therefore, be negative; we must support goodness wherever we find it. Wherever there are agencies working for peace, wherever as in our time agencies like the United Nations attempt to bring about reconciliation, there we know that some of the light from the Kingdom of God has fallen. Because this is God's history, we must at the same time be criticizers of injustice and supporters of the good, wherever we find either of them. We know that this world belongs to God and that in his faithfulness we can trust. With Him who has taken us into his confidence we look toward that world which is both coming and yet already here.

"Then I saw a new heaven and a new earth; for the first heaven and the first earth had passed away, and the sea was no more. And I saw the holy city, new Jerusalem, coming down out of heaven from God, prepared as a bride adorned for her husband; and I heard a great voice from the throne saying, 'Behold, the dwelling of God is with men. He will dwell with them, and they shall be his people, and God himself will be with them; he will wipe away every tear from their eyes, and death shall be no more, neither shall there be mourning nor crying nor pain any more, for the former things have passed away.'" (Rev. 21:1-4.)

UNDERSTANDING THE BIBLE

In this fresh and thought-provoking approach to the study of the Bible by laymen, Mr. Denbeaux catches our interest by relating the story of the Bible to the story of our personal lives. He makes the covenant-faith of the Old Testament and the renewal of that faith through Jesus Christ in the New Testament important to us in the twentieth century. In each of us there is an Abraham, a Moses, a David, a Jeremiah, a Peter, a Paul, and a John. These men are ourselves and they struggle with our problems—and the answers they find have meaning for us. As we read this book, the Bible becomes exciting and we turn to it with eagerness to find out what the Word of God has to say to us.

QUESTIONS FOR DISCUSSION

Discussion I. Chapter 1. "A Serious Plea for Lay Scholarship." Protestantism requires that we study the Bible carefully. 1. How can a misreading of the Bible shut God up as "an idler in heaven"? 2. In what sense is the Bible "unreadable"? 3. What "discipline" is required if we are to understand the Bible? 4. Why cannot the Protestant delegate the study and understanding of the Bible to ministers, evangelists, or specialists? 5. In what way is Protestantism a "hard," rather than a "soft," faith?

Discussion II. Chapter 2. "The Tools of Biblical Study." Certain skills must be developed in order to understand the Bible. 1. What is the basic meaning of the word "criticism"? 2. How does criticism make the mind come alive? 3. What questions ought one to ask as he begins to study one of the books in the Bible? 4. Through whose eyes do we see the stories of Abraham and Moses? 5. Why is it important to know the historical facts surrounding any particular Biblical passage? 6. Is it important to understand the way in which words are used? 7. What is the relationship between truth and legend or myth? 8. Why is the study of the Bible necessary for the creation of the community which is called the church?

Discussion III. Chapter 3. "The Church Tries to Understand What God Has Done." The ways in which the various branches of the church understand the Bible are different. 1. How do the churches "alternate between trembling creatureliness and pretentious conviction"? 2. What is the danger in the Catholic position with its emphasis upon tradition, liturgy, and the sacraments? How does this affect a study of the Bible? 3. What has Protestantism to learn from this Catholic position? 4. Why is Protestantism "the champion of a faith centered in the Bible"? 5. How do we distinguish between God's word and human interpretations? 6. What is the central assurance of the Bible for Protestants? 7. How would you describe the "Sectarian conscience"? What is its strength? its weakness? 8. How does the "principle of selectivity" undermine true Bible study? 9. How can we combine the insights of Catholicism, Protestantism, and Sectarianism in understanding the Bible?

Discussion IV. Chapter 4. "The Words of Man and the Word of God." There are three participants in the covenant: God, Abraham, and you. 1. How do God and man communicate? 2. How do words change relationships between people? 3. What is the nature of the specific word that God speaks to men in the Old Testament? 4. In what does "man's true hope" rest? 5. What is meant by saying that what a man *does* comes out of what he *is?* 6. How does the Bible understand sin? 7. How does God keep faith with us? 8. What is the relationship between God's acceptance of us and our trust in him? 9. How is "Abraham" related to each of us? (Comment on Deuteronomy 5:3) 10. What has a "wilderness experience" to do with our grasping the meaning of God's word?

Discussion V. Chapter 5. "An Ancient Story Which Is Our Story." The story of the Hebrew people is also our story. 1. How did events and conditions in the days of Solomon cause a man to write about the Tower of Babel, the Garden of Eden, the murder of Abel, the destruction of Sodom, the exodus from Egypt, and the golden calf? 2. What events and conditions in *our* day drive us to reconsider the ancient stories of the Old Testament? 3. Why is human freedom always in danger of being lost? 4. What makes it possible for us to endure freedom? 5. What has the exodus of the Hebrew slaves from Egypt to do with us today? 6. Why is it that the way to freedom is a "lonely journey each man must make for himself"? 7. What is "creatureliness"? What is its relationship to freedom? 8. Why is it important for us not to fear humiliation? 9. How can the church renew the covenant-faith in our day?

Discussion VI. Chapter 6. "Re-Creation and Renewal." God's power is even now available for the healing of men and of nations. 1. Why cannot man fully understand God? Why is mystery necessary? 2. Why is it heretical "to substitute the familiar voice of Jesus for the uncertain voice of the Holy Stranger"? 3. Why must Christian faith always remain involved in "this world"? 4. Which view is more in line with the New Testament—to see Jesus as the fulfillment of our hopes or to see him as the abandonment of hope? 5. Just what is the "offense" of Jesus? 6. How does human pride keep us from understanding God? 7. What is the relationship between human dignity and our difficulty in grasping the meaning of God as revealed in Christ? 8. Why is it that within a true disciple of Jesus "belief and unbelief eternally struggle"? 9. Are we willing to admit that *"we* are politely, but nevertheless unutterably, opposed to the Kingdom of God"? 10. What is the power by which the broken relationship between God and man is renewed? 11. What has the resurrection of Jesus Christ to do with the renewal of this broken relationship?

Study Suggestions

This book may be studied in six sessions or in three. If it is decided to use only three sessions, it would be best to discuss Chs. 1, 2, and 3 at the first meeting; Chs. 4 and 5 at the second; and Ch. 6, with the Epilogue, at the third. If the group is large, a stimulating method for these discussions would be to divide into small groups of six or seven each and have them study the text and find the answers to the questions before coming together in one large group to report their findings and to ask further questions. At all times, remember that this book is not an end in itself—but a means to stir up individual interest in reading the Bible intelligently.

This Study Guide was prepared by John W. Van Zanten, minister, The Roslyn Presbyterian Church, Roslyn, New York